The Education *of a* Trial Lawyer

Gerald J. Todaro

ABA
AMERICAN BAR ASSOCIATION
Senior Lawyers Division

Cover design by Elizabeth Kulak/ABA Design

All persons mentioned in this book are or were real individuals, but most names apart from friends, partners, and deceased persons—those of plaintiffs and defendants, their attorneys (excepting Charlie Brown and Don Reuben), physicians and physician experts, and judges—have been changed to respect their privacy. This book reflects the author's present recollections of experiences over time. Some events have been compressed, and some dialogue has been recreated.

Printed in the United States of America.

30 29 28 27 26   5 4 3 2 1

ISBN 978-1-63905-730-6

To my high school soulmates Paul Scott and
Frankie Ray who gave me certainty.

To my children Ashley and Brady who never complained
when my work interfered with their life.

For my wife dedicated to making me a better person.

I want to thank Allison Williams and Dinty Moore.
Without their guidance and encouragement this book
would never have entered the portals of a bookstore.

"The life of the law has not been logic: it has been experience."

The Common Law,
Oliver Wendel Holmes Jr.

"You'll still find me in the library looking for luck at 3 o'clock in the morning."

Louis Nizer

"I have never seen a major trial which lacked significant perjury, and I have yet to see that perjury punished."

F. Lee Bailey

Contents

Prologue

It was late Friday afternoon and the jury had been deliberating since noon. The foreperson had just passed a folded sheet of paper to the bailiff. The note to the judge requested the transcript of Dr. Miller's testimony. The jury wanted to hear his explanation about why the patient died on the operating table. Acid percolated in my stomach. I knew that some of the jurors would struggle with exonerating Dr. Jack Miller from the death of a 25-year-old mother with two little children.

The dead patient's angry husband demanded answers and wanted money—a lot of money. His wife had undergone a routine gallbladder procedure, supposedly a 45-minute surgery. Two hours went by before the surgeon finally appeared in the family waiting room. "I couldn't save her," he said. "Jennifer is gone."

No one dies from gallbladder surgery unless the doctor is negligent—this was the opening salvo from the family's dapper lawyer's first day in the courtroom. Sitting next to Jack Miller at the lawyer's table, I could feel his anxiety. His shoulders hunched and his jaw clenched every time the plaintiff's lawyer accused him of ignoring techniques of safe gallbladder surgery. I had my game face on. No matter how damning the accusations, I maintained my obligatory composed and unruffled demeanor. Inside, though, it hurt to hear staccato sound bites about young daughters growing up without their mother, never sharing birthdays or mother-daughter secrets or hugs of joy at graduations, or the excitement of planning baby showers. After the plaintiff lawyer's opening statement, I wanted to grab the lawyer's neck and choke him until he stopped breathing. I don't think I've ever said that out loud before, but this anger started when I transitioned to defending physicians instead of suing them.

My client wasn't the only one bleeding emotionally. The female bailiff took me aside on the third day of trial and drew close to my ear, whispering that Jack's wife would slip away to the courthouse bathroom during recess, sit in a stall, and cry.

The judge read the jury's request to the court reporter to preserve the question on the trial court record, then narrowed her eyes, and hastily scribbled her answer: "The jury must rely on their collective memory of Doctor Miller's testimony." It was 4:00 Friday afternoon; the judge had children to pick up from grade school. The bailiff delivered the judge's response to the jurors waiting impatiently in the jury room.

Jack and I sat on an unpadded church pew bench outside the courtroom. Jack asked why the jury wanted his testimony. It's not unusual, I said. Someone is hung up on a piece of evidence and reading the actual testimony would clear up the confusion. If the jury had asked for the plaintiff's expert testimony explaining why he was negligent, I told him, that would mean trouble for us.

The question for the jury was simple, but finding the truth is an elusive endeavor for non-medical people serving on juries. Did the young patient die from negligence, or an unavoidable but rare complication of a routine gallbladder procedure? The answer depends on *what version of the truth* the jury believes. In medical malpractice cases, the lawyers on both sides hire medical experts hailing from prestigious academic medical institutions. During the second day of trial, the plaintiff's medial expert, Dr. McVie, a graduate of Yale Medical School, displayed an anatomical drawing of the blood supply around the gallbladder to explain how the negligent insertion of a trocar caused bleeding. Dr. Miller and our medical experts countered with an explanation of how a rare, unavoidable injury to a small blood vessel could lead to death. But would the jury listen? Would they overcome their heartfelt feelings for a young husband left with two kids and no wife and send them home with no money? The jury received an instruction from the judge not to allow sympathy to interfere in their deliberations. Blocking empathy for human suffering, especially when it comes to children, strains the mental will of jurors, yet most will do it. It is not unusual to see some jurors cry during the testimony of a parent who lost a young child.

On the fourth day of trial, I called Jack to the witness stand. As instructed over hours of woodshedding, he eyeballed the jury and explained how at the start of the procedure, he made a small incision in the skin over the abdomen, then used a specialized tube (trocar) with a transparent tip to allow him to visualize the layers of the abdominal wall as he accessed the abdominal cavity. Once he gained access, he inserted an illuminated telescope to inspect the abdominal cavity. After surveying the abdominal organs, he infused carbon dioxide into the abdomen to expand it so he could better visualize adjacent organs and vessels, look for any injury, and safely remove the gallbladder. Any injury to organs or vessels usually occurs during this initial procedure because it's a blind entry—doctors cannot see ahead of the tube as it clears fat and muscle tissue. All the experts, both plaintiff and defense, had made this point earlier in the trial. This point was the prelude to what happened next.

When Dr. Miller introduced the miniature camera into Jennifer's abdomen, he told the jury he had noticed a small speck of blood—not usually alarming. He started carefully dissecting the surrounding tissue to free up the gallbladder. Suddenly, the heart tracing on the monitor hooked up to Jennifer danced wildly. Then it went flat. Dr. Miller and the anesthesiologist were stunned, but after a quick analysis of the potential causes, they suspected an air embolus—a bubble of air—stopped the heart. The trocar had hit a vein and opened a small hole that allowed a carbon dioxide bubble to travel up the vein leading to the heart. The air bubble blocked blood flow. "We tried everything to dislodge the blockage, even repositioning the operating table to lower the head as much as possible," Jack said. After an uncomfortable pause, he shifted side to side, looking away from the jury. "Nothing worked." His tone was remorseful. Dr. Miller couldn't hide his anguish over Jennifer's death. Jennifer was the daughter of his friend, a rounding nurse of 20 years.

The entire week, the plaintiff's counsel and his experts had battled with me over the significance of a speckle of blood. I told the jury that a speckle of blood was not unusual and not unexpected when tunneling through the muscle and tissue layers of the abdominal wall. In *my version of the truth,* I argued, a small amount of blood was not uncommon—nothing to indicate that a blood vessel had been injured. The plaintiff's lawyers claimed a careful surgeon would have immediately recognized that the defect in the vein raised the risk of an air embolus. By this time in my career, I finally understood human angst in the face of the limitations of knowledge and understanding. We humans can look at the same set of facts and come to completely opposite conclusions. One of our cognitive shortcuts that gets us into trouble lies in the assumptions we make when the true nature of events is beyond our grasp.

Here is where trial lawyers step in to fill in the gaps of what juries cannot understand because of their lack of medical experience. We have honed the craft of hindsight analysis to give new meaning to the course of events. Once lawyers know the outcome, they attach more importance to an isolated fact that previously didn't seem important or meaningful. Trial lawyers will feed off the misconception that a past event was more predictable than it actually was. Juries are unaware of the fallacy of "selective attention," but they should be. Hindsight made that insignificant speck of blood a red flag warning of danger.

During final arguments, the plaintiff's lawyers were painfully persuasive, using the subtle deception of hindsight analysis to sway the jury. They worked backward from the death of the patient, connecting the dots from a cardiac arrythmia caused by blocked blood flow, caused by an air bubble, caused by a small hole in a vein caused by Dr. Miller's negligent injury to the vein. Skilled plaintiff's lawyers who have perfected retrospective scope analysis use several analogies to pummel juries to the conclusion that an insignificant detail was, in fact, a clear warning. The plaintiff's lawyers hammered Jack. That small amount of blood was a red flag, a caution light at a busy intersection, a stop sign mandating a halt of moving forward. In hindsight, the jury no longer viewed a speck of blood as insignificant; now they saw it as a warning of a pending catastrophe. It was just common sense, the plaintiffs argued. Dr. Miller should have recognized that he had injured a blood vessel and that the potential of an air embolus could kill the patient. He should have removed the laparoscope and performed an open procedure, eliminating the need for CO_2, and Jennifer would have gone home to her husband and two children that evening.

Dr. McVie mentioned that the surgery wasn't indicated in the first place, according to her emphatic husband, because Jennifer's symptoms were not that bad (an afterthought allegation I forgot to address in my final argument to the jury).

Twenty minutes had passed since the jury had asked to hear more evidence. Suddenly, the bailiff poked her head outside the courtroom door. "The jury has a verdict." My stomach squeezed to the size of an egg. For a moment I was back in high school, outside the principal's office. Whose version of the truth would the jury believe?

After five agonizing minutes sitting in the courtroom while the judge reviewed the jury verdict and checked the necessary signatures on the jury forms, she announced, "Verdict for the defendant." Jack gasped in relief from his pent-up pain and frustration.

Once the jury is discharged from their duties, the lawyers can discuss the case with the jury. As I walked out of the courthouse, I saw the plaintiff's lawyer talking with one of the jurors on the courthouse steps. I could see him gesturing, apparently in frustration. I called him a week later to find out what the juror had to say. "Unbelievable," he said. The jury thought the husband lied. He had testified that his wife's symptoms were not as bad as Dr. Miller claimed. His testimony was backed up by the pathology report that found only sludge in the gallbladder, but no gallstones. The jury thought he had exaggerated. I congratulated him for trying a good case and hung up quickly.

In hindsight, the most compelling moment during the trial was Jack's response to the plaintiff's lawyer grilling him on his lack of skill and ripping a hole in the vein. Jack slumped more noticeably with each accusatory question. Finally, Jack jerked upright. "I'm sorry," he said, his voice trembling. "I'm not perfect." I observed a couple of jurors react. He had touched a soft spot in human DNA—affection and forgiveness for someone who is trying their hardest, but who has stumbled. Despite the highly qualified medical experts, despite science, logic, and compelling medical facts, empathy conquered the minds of the jury—the jury empathized with Jack more than they did with the plaintiff.

This book's title, *The Education of a Trial Lawyer*, comes from a trial lawyer's life that played out like a chess game in a stressful, combative environment, in full view of jurors and judges. All of us are flawed by the human condition, and the risk of mistakes and poor judgment rises when confronted with uncertainty and performing under stress. This is the unseen gamesmanship in the courtroom that seasoned lawyers play with an eye on jury persuasion. This memoir contains stories of high-stakes litigation and intentional manipulation of the limitations of the human condition. You will not find this explained or taught in law school or appreciate it unless you're educated on the subtle illusions of histrionics and the spoken word. Through actual cases, I will examine the black holes awaiting participants, judges, and jurors searching for the truth, including the uncertainty in medicine and unpredictable outcomes; witnesses under stress; the deception of hindsight; disinformation from so-called experts schooled in telling the truth attractively; the mistrust of science; the negative influence of financial incentives; mediocre judges; and the danger of pure evil. However, on occasion, no amount of evidence will persuade jurors with righteous, deep-seated beliefs and personal truths that are incompatible with your client's plea for justice.

Legal scholars extoll the virtue of the courtroom as the crucible of truth, justice, and the cutting edge of democracy—a place where villains are found guilty and tortfeasors are held accountable. But I see a fishbowl of mercenary combatants twisting reality and trying to blame someone for the costly mess of human failure—a place where the virtues of the human soul are checked at the door. Human nature plays by its own rules, and fairness is not one of them.

1 Law School: You're Never the Same Again

Lesson 1: Don't take anything spoken or written at face value. Facts are paramount in reasoning.

Law professors like to say that law school changes the way you look at the world. To me, it's more about seeing anew the vulnerability of the human condition. Historians tell us that history repeats itself, and people have repeated the same errors in human judgment since Adam and Eve allegedly tasted the forbidden fruit. Most lawyers don't spend a lot of time reading history. Instead, we read case law, a collection of judicial decisions that use legal principles to resolve interpersonal disputes involving money and compensation for injury or economic losses. On criminal matters, protection of the constitutional rights of the accused are under the microscope. Lawyers know that people make a mess of their lives and the lives of others. But how do lawyers learn to use legal principles to resolve thousands of disputes that clog our courts weekly? This skill is known as "thinking like a lawyer." If asked, I couldn't give a succinct definition of the criteria for thinking like a lawyer; however, from a trial lawyer's perspective, we are trained to isolate concrete facts, appreciate the difference between hard facts and assumptions and opinions, apply legal principles of evidence and procedure, and rely on the law and the logical force of evidence to counter the arguments of our opponent. In every trial there is a giant chessboard in the courtroom, with evidence moving like chess pieces to checkmate the arguments of the opposing lawyer. Thinking like a lawyer playing a game of chess is key. And lawyers, by the nature of their personality, are competitive, but to survive in the courtroom, trial lawyers must be *fiercely* competitive. Trial lawyers are paid to win.

Justice is for winners.

My law school's core curriculum was similar to most students that enter an accredited law school, yet the environment was unusual, and many of my fellow students had been turned down by the more prestigious law schools. Capital University Law School began as a part-time evening law school in 1903, sponsored by a national program making legal education possible and affordable. The Columbus Law School met at the local YMCA in downtown Columbus, Ohio. By the time I entered the full-time program in 1971, the law school had moved to the upscale Columbus suburb of Bexley and was affiliated with Capital University, a small, expensive, private liberal arts college. The former showroom for a car dealership, a large concrete-block building painted bright white, built on a busy four-lane main drag through Bexley, was repurposed as a law library and housed the law school's administrative offices. Within a week of my first semester, a third-year student told us that only 16 percent of his class had survived. My first two years were something akin to a sweatshop. In years past, Capital had a 100 percent passage rate on the Ohio bar. At the time I graduated, Capital Law School students had the highest passage rate of any Ohio law school on the Ohio bar exam, and an American Bar Association survey listed Capital as having one of the highest acceptance rates in the country.

I will never forget my interview with Assistant Dean Palmer in his chimney-sized office, a twelve-by-six drywall cubicle with a metal desk and two chairs. When I closed the door to his office, the white acoustic ceiling panels lifted off the metal frames. As expected, his first question was, "Why should we let you in here? "I defended my low LSAT score with the standard response of the day: "I'm not good at taking standardized tests." I told Palmer that the dean of the University of Tennessee Law School liked the meteoric improvement of my grades, and if I applied to UT, I would have been accepted, but after five years in Knoxville, I needed a change of scenery. I should mention that "meteoric" might have been a slight exaggeration; it was more like a pub crawl. Dean Palmer didn't blink; he said nothing, but I thought I saw a slight facial twitch. He asked where else I had applied. Failing to notice the elegantly framed law school diploma behind his desk, I mentioned the University of Michigan.

After another pause, he brandished a smirk. "You couldn't smell the University of Michigan."

The year was 1971. I faced professors Turack and Sullivan, who were intent on spitting out my soul—gatekeepers turning away those mentally unfit for admission into the legal fraternity. The memory of these two professors still lives in my head. The Socratic method used by Professor Turack, aka "the Turk," was an experience that felt like being dragged by a horse over a mile of broken glass. Dan Turack was a scholar. He'd earned a doctorate of judicial science from the University of Michigan, a degree reserved for aspiring academics. Law professors with an SJD from a top ten law school were usually hired at the Ivies or the University of Chicago, not Capital. What was he doing here teaching Contracts? No one I know has ever had the nerve to ask.

"The Turk" wasn't a mean man, but his absolute refusal to broach ignorance in his classroom was a nightmare of humbling experiences. In class, he stood hawk-eyed behind the lectern. He was clean shaven, just under six feet tall, dressed in his customary black suit, starched white shirt, and narrow dark tie, his jet-black hair combed straight back. He peppered students with hypothetical questions that scrambled the original facts of an assigned case, turning the logic of the legal conclusions into a puzzle missing half the pieces. Memorization counted for nothing. The Turk demanded students apply the law of a specific case to fresh sets of facts. Occasionally, a student's logical, reasoned conclusion brought a faint smile to one side of Turack's mouth. Halley's Comet comes around more often. To this day, I still remember the Turk's classic response to dumb answers: a frosty "NOhhhhhhhhh," and then on to the next victim. He never came right out and said we didn't belong. "Some of you," Turack would say, "will be working for Standard Oil someday."

I got it. I'd be pumping gas for a living.

If there is a hell, the Turk will be there teaching Contracts.

Another pedagogue in the rare species department was our Torts professor, John Sullivan. Torts is the study of laws assessing monetary compensation for negligent (wrongful) conduct. Like Contracts, Torts is core curriculum for first-year law students. John Sullivan (everyone called him Sully behind his back) differed from Turack in style and pedigree.

Sullivan graduated from Western Reserve University Law School in Cleveland (now named Case Western University School of Law). He looked older than his 49 years. To describe him as portly was charitable. Sully was five-foot-five with a prominent belly. A lima bean with metal-framed eyeglasses wrapped in an undersized checkered sportscoat comes to mind.

He wore rumpled short-sleeved shirts accessorized with neckties—the narrow end hanging below the wider end. Inevitably, the wider end twisted to the front, presenting a Sears and Roebuck label. Sullivan was an acquired taste. He had the startling habit of darting to one side of the room mid-sentence. He paced constantly and coughed incessantly. When he coughed, his tongue protruded from his mouth, forming a perfect U shape. We joked that you needed a bib if you sat in the front row.

Where Turack relied on the Socratic method, forcing the mind to consider alternative arguments, Sullivan lectured on black-letter law—the well-established legal rules that are no longer subject to reasonable dispute—and how fundamental principles of law governed the outcome of each case. Turack reacted to ignorance with contempt; Sullivan responded with anger. Turack used hypotheticals to change the facts, challenging our presumptions and understanding of legal principles; Sullivan assigned case after case tracking the application of one principle of law and how new and different facts changed the outcome. Turack trained law students to solve legal problems and recognize the complexity of legal disputes; Sullivan drilled law students on the nuts and bolts of the legal subjects on the Ohio bar exam.

Sullivan beamed as he passed out reading assignments: case citations and law review articles for us to hunt down in the law library to incorporate in our outlines. Sully's list often filled a page and a half of legal-sized paper. He delighted in entertaining us, but any perceived gesture of disrespect triggered his wrath. I remember a guttural wheeze trailing Sullivan's first handout of extra reading material as it made its way around the classroom on a Friday morning. Sully reacted like a patient shocked by a defibrillator. His body lurched forward, endangering the students in the front row. Red in the face and spitting his words, he ranted about mediocrity and middle-management types. "If the work is too hard," he said, "you don't belong here."

Sully's teaching method stretched the mental landscape of a principle of law. Take, for example, the Last Clear Chance Doctrine: best explained as which driver had the last opportunity to avoid an accident. Unlike Turack, Sully assigned multiple cases applying the legal theory of Last Clear Chance, gave us law review articles interpreting the theory, and lectured instead of calling out hypotheticals. If a law student read the cases and additional reading assignments and synthesized his lectures into an outline, even yours truly could learn to apply legal principles to any set of new facts.

Not until I started trying civil cases for big money did I truly appreciate the difference in the teaching styles of Turack and Sullivan. Turack exhorted the examination of all sides of a problem. Sullivan sermonized on the need to make a definitive decision. He flunked one of my good friends because he used "weasel words" (circling words) in his answer, such as "I believe," "possibly," or "could be." As I've mentioned, trials are almost always a chess match—the trial attorney is the grand master, moving the chess pieces of evidence (soft and hard facts) to advance their theories and block the validity and persuasiveness of their opponent's evidence. After I formulated the theories in my case, I forced myself to think through how my adversary would put their case together. Sometimes in a civil case, I could present two or three claims for the plaintiff, but I learned that focusing the jury on one theory of recovery in court produced better results.

There's always a "but" in trial work. Despite meticulous preparations, witnesses disappoint—or worse, they concede arguments that nearly defeat your case. Or the judge may throw out important evidence, ignoring prevailing case law. Surprises at trial are the norm. Anticipating everything that can go wrong is impossible. Years ago, I was defending a general surgeon in a death case. My star expert was a full professor and chairman of the department of a major academic medical center, and a board examiner for young doctors sitting for board certification as a general surgeon—compelling evidence of the expert's credibility. After my direct examination, the plaintiff's counsel asked the doctor about a federal court decision excluding his opinion because it was false and unreliable. I immediately objected. We took a short recess to allow me to read the decision, which involved two reports written by my expert. Despite my vehement arguments, the court overruled my objections and permitted the plaintiff's lawyer to reveal that a judge in a previous case had excluded my expert's testimony because it was unreliable. On redirect, I had my expert explain to the jury that the second report added new opinions based on new information from discovery. We talked to the jury after a verdict for my client. I asked how the evidence of the federal court decision affected their opinion of my expert. "You didn't seem bothered by it, so it wasn't that important," they said. A witness's emotional demeanor on the witness stand impacts jurors, and so does the trial lawyer's demeanor.

Trial work is stressful, and there are emotionally charged moments that can overwhelm one's composure and disable clear thinking. In the words of Mike Tyson, "Everyone has a plan until they get punched in the face." Wearing a game face and maintaining emotional cool is an indispensable skill often acquired in high school or college sports. I have to confess, it's not easy to stay calm when you have a harpoon sticking out of your chest.

As we go forward, one of the themes of this book is the unseen and underappreciated realities in the courtroom; that is, the impact of the human condition on the outcome of jury trials.

2 Meet Billy Pollitt and Paul Scott

Lesson 2: Lawyering is a skill business, and mastering the skills depends more on hard work than scores on standardized tests.

During my first semester in law school, I didn't sleep well. I had to master a mental exercise that required law students to perform four steps: learn the legal principle, prioritize relevant facts, apply the principle of law to the facts, then make a logical conclusion explaining why the rule of law controlled the outcome. I grasped this new mindset. But what kept me up at night was my low LSAT score that predicted I would do poorly in law school.

Permit me now to introduce two young men whose friendship and influence elevated my cognitive discipline to a level that empowered me to excel in law school and the practice of law. Early that fall, in one of the makeshift cubicles in the law library next to me, sat H. William Pollitt, hunkering over a law book, wearing an oversized Ohio State football jersey. Billy had played on Ohio State's national championship football team in 1968, and in the Rose Bowl in 1969. Ohio State's law school rejected him, despite the university's legendary football coach Woody Hayes pleading Billy's case to the dean of admissions. The problem? Billy had low LSAT scores, and his grades were marginal. "A rhesus monkey could have scored higher on the LSAT," Billy told me in his endearing, unabashed style. By Billy's calculation, we were both neck-and-neck with a primate.

Billy gave me snippets of his five-minute interview with Assistant Dean Palmer. Billy stood six feet two inches, and his playing weight was about 225 pounds. He had added a few since then. Billy gracefully stuffed his body into a chair he said was made for midgets, and waited for what he thought would be a breezy interview, since Coach Hayes had called the dean of Capital Law School and the decision for his admission was a done deal. After a few pleasantries about Ohio State football, Palmer had asked Billy if he was good with his hands. Billy looked down and studied the palms of his hand. He thought Palmer must be testing him—could he think on his feet?

"Give me a knife, a fork, and a buffet, and I'm a bitch," Billy had said.

"That's good," Palmer replied. "Maybe you should go to hospitality school." Before Billy said another word, Palmer added, "You're wasting my time and your time."

Billy tracked down Coach Hayes. He knew where to find him: in the film room breaking down game films of next year's opponents. As Billy tells it, the exchange went like this:

"Do you want to go to law school?" Woody yelled, six inches from Billy's face.

"Yeah, Coach."

"Will you make it?"

"Yeah, I can do it," Billy replied boldly, knowing that even a hint of doubt would rile Coach Hayes.

"You better, or you'll end up screwing over yourself and everyone behind you. My word won't mean s---." (Like most of Woody's boys, H. William Pollitt, even decades after Woody's death, pulled back before saying anything disrespectful of his legendary coach.)

Despite our instant kinship, there was a major difference between me and Mr. Pollitt. I feared failure and rejection. Billy, undaunted, embraced the challenge. Acquiring the mental skill to process contradictory facts and competing legal principles is an uphill battle for most first-semester law students. However, the first time Billy responded to the Turk, his uphill climb seemed as formidable as scaling Mt. Everest without oxygen.

Turack: "Mr. Pollitt, please give us the facts and holding in *Smith v. Jones* and explain the court's decision."

Billy: "Well, ya know there's these two guys. John and this other dude. John asked the other dude to make him a table. The dude said OK, but I need money to buy supplies and stuff. John gave him some cash; the dude took the money but bought himself a watch—screwed over John. Never made the table like he said he would. So, John sued him."

"Oh, shit," the guy next to me whispered. The Turk wasted no time.

"Mr. Pollitt, you're in law school, not a high school social studies class." Turack always addressed us by our last names.

"You will think and talk like a lawyer; you *will* use legalese or stay out of my classroom."

The Turk demanded we use the language of the law to make legal arguments. Billy should have raised questions about whether there was an *offer*, a *promise* of *performance*, an *acceptance* and *consideration* (a consideration is something of value returned for an item or service). Scandalized by Billy's performance, Turack glared at Billy. The few seconds it took our professor to call on another victim seemed like eternity.

I remember thinking, no way would H. William Pollitt make grades in law school. But Billy seemed immune to Turack. And, as I later learned, he was also immune to self-doubt. In his mind, there was no challenge he couldn't overcome. Coach Hayes was the constant voice in his head. After the law library closed at midnight, Billy often drove me to my apartment in his pickup truck, reciting inspirational quotes from Woody. My favorite: "There ain't a horse that can't be rode, and there ain't a rider that can't be throwed."

That fall, Billy treated every day as if it were the week before The Game: Ohio State versus The State Up North (for the uninitiated, that would be the University of Michigan). He recorded Turack's lectures and listened to the tapes in his dorm room. He outlined class notes, saying it helped him to learn how Turack's mind worked. He didn't just learn the facts of a case and the legal principles controlling the outcome; he mastered them.

"JT," he said to me on the way home one night, "you gotta hit 'til the whistle blows."

***

Paul O. Scott. Scott—no one used his first name—was quick with a quip, colorful, and entertaining. Scott was a full-time law student and worked long hours at the Ohio Senate as a page to pay tuition. In afternoon classes, Scott dozed off. His class notes were nonexistent. But he sucked the law off anyone who would talk with him. We sat next to each other in the front row of Professor Freeman's Constitutional Law class. Only the front row seats were open if you were late to class, and Scott was always late for his afternoon classes. Inevitably, 20 minutes into Freeman's lecture, Scott's head bobbed. His head would slowly dip forward, then snap upright, a perfect rendition of a chicken pecking the ground. Bets were placed on how long before the chicken would roost. I'd spend two hours scribbling notes, poking Scott, hoping to avoid Freeman's wrath. Freeman had missed his calling. He should have pursued a medical career as an anesthesiologist. His lectures were better than anesthesia.

Scott would set the standard that became an enduring cognitive habit for my small circle of friends—the rule against uncertainty. His mental discipline purged the natural impulse to speak before thinking, before analyzing, before knowing. If Scott called me about the holding in case assigned the next day in class, and I began the sentence with "I think," or "I believe," he cut me off immediately. "Know your facts, know the law," he'd harp. Eventually, the catch in my throat was his voice in my head: "Do you know for sure, or are you guessing?"

The day before the Torts exam, Scott showed up at my apartment around two in the afternoon, carrying his pristine torts textbook. He used the receipt as a bookmark. The first run-through of my torts outline took about eight hours. My outline was 12 double-sided pages of legal principles, facts, and case holdings on a yellow legal pad. We anticipated Sully creating unfamiliar fact patterns to conceal the applicable law. So, I peppered Scott with fact scenarios, trying to disguise the controlling legal principle.

We finished the second run-through of my outline at 2:00 a.m. The exam was scheduled for 9:00 a.m.

"Scott, we are done," I said, exhaling loudly for emphasis.

"No, we're not," Scott said, "we've got to go through it one more time. We need to know this stuff cold."

I boiled more water for instant coffee.

Grades were posted after Christmas break—no names, only numbers on the grade sheet tacked to a wall in the foyer of the law library. Unlike law schools with burnished reputations, Capital didn't believe in grade inflation. C was a solid grade. I searched for the Torts grade sheet. I saw lots of Cs and some Ds and a few Fs. When I saw a B+ next to my number, I reached into my pocket and checked my number. I wanted to run outside and make snow angels in the parking lot. Silently I screamed, "Hell, I'm a genius! *I am a genius.*"

Thanks to a sweatshop of a law school, Billy, Scott, and two terrifying professors, I had learned to embrace and maintain a maximum level of effort, focus, and discipline—an elite performance level that would pay big dividends in the future. Back in law school, I didn't appreciate the value of Scott and Billy's friendship as much as I do now. Hitching my brain to Scott and Billy's fact-driven mindset shaped my identity as a successful trial lawyer. These two unique and driven individuals were more important to me than my LSAT scores and the law school I graduated from. They lifted me to a level of performance that I would never have achieved on my own. What is scary about my evolution, though, is the random way in which it happened. I couldn't get accepted to a highly regarded law school, and I could have sat next to guys in class that worked just hard enough to get through. If not for the disciplined mental acuity of Scott and Billy, I could have buckled when Turack made it clear to me, after I got a C in his course, that I was wasting my time in law school.

3 Minding the Gaffe in the Courtroom

Lesson 3: Jurors ignore the law when it is inconsistent with their personal values.

In the spring of my last year of law school, I clerked in a law firm for a lawyer who was a political operative in the Franklin County Republican Party in Columbus, Ohio. At my insistence, he arranged a job interview with the Franklin County Prosecutor. Before going back to law school, I visited a high school friend in New York City who went to law school at Columbia University. He took me to his Evidence class, taught by Irving Younger, who delivered his lectures as dramatically as a Shakespearean actor. He urged the class to master the rules of evidence if they aspired to be trial lawyers. The class was fascinating. I decided I wanted to be a trial lawyer.

The day I was sworn in as an Assistant Franklin County Prosecutor on the felony trial staff, I elbowed my way past lawyers who had paid their dues presenting cases to the grand jury and working up cases in the Juvenile Division. The prosecutor who hired me was running for a judgeship, and while I was a legal intern waiting for the bar results, I spent nights and weekends helping him on his judicial campaign. I unabashedly followed the advice of the political insider that got me the interview: I did what I was asked to do. And kept my mouth shut. I put up campaign signs and handed out literature in smoky bowling alleys and at local business picnics and public events. I wanted to be a trial lawyer, and I wanted it now. Politics, it turns out, squelches credentials.

Political influence is muscle. I saw nothing unfair about leapfrogging my way to the felony staff. In the future, though, I'd experience how politics dumbs down the legal system, especially candidates for judicial office.

During my first six months, the night before most of my trials, I would call the chief prosecutor, Jim O'Grady. Jim's rise in the prosecutor's office was hypersonic. Jim grew up in the Bronx; he was a classic New Yorker, and besides his love for the Yankees, as the saying goes, he didn't suffer fools gladly. He'd bite your head off for a stupid question. His instinct for the jugular was rattlesnake quick, likely due to his boyhood days playing poker and navigating the perilous streets and alleys of the Bronx. Besides his signature skill of cross-examining psychiatrists who testified that the defendant was insane at the time of a murder, Jim could engage any juror during jury selection as if they were sitting in a bar stool next to him or chatting at a church social function. While in his office one late afternoon between trials, he raised the subject of jury selection, specifically my cumbersome attempts to pick jurors. I was 28 years old, and my social skills dipped to the level of a late-night B movie—always good for a chuckle Saturday morning in the office after my Friday night adventures at singles bars.

The gaffes during jury selection were piling up like dead mice on my doorstep. The latest was a young woman who worked at Chemical Abstracts, a large company in Columbus that provided resources for chemical information. "How long have you been working as a secretary?" I asked. "No," she said, "I have a PhD in Chemical Engineering." Awkward silence followed. There is another rebuke I still recall. I asked a married woman if she worked. "Yes, I work. I have three children," she said. "I'm up at sunrise, I dress the children, make their breakfast, drive one of them to preschool, read to the youngest, wash clothes, call the plumber, take the children to their doctor appointments, take my oldest to gymnastics school, make dinner, get the kids to bed, and spend a few minutes with my husband after the kids are in bed. Does that count?"

Trust me on this: I have never asked a woman those two questions again, inside or outside the courtroom.

Jim didn't mention I was naïve, but my fellow prosecutors were not so diplomatic. In one of our informal training sessions, I was advised to stop asking jurors if they could be fair. During jury selection, after I got a little information about a juror's education and work history, I asked if the juror "could be fair," and almost every juror said yes. So I stopped asking questions and moved on to the next juror. I was leaving individuals on the jury who presented a reasonable possibility that they were anti-government, anti-police, or bucked authority. Jim told me to spend more time finding out more about how jurors make a living. I learned to search for jurors whose jobs, backgrounds, and personal experiences implied that they looked to the police for protection and were inclined to give my police officer and victims the benefit of the doubt. Long-haired guys with beards were the first excused. My assumption was that such individuals were suspicious of authority and the police.

No lawyer with significant experience fully trusts jurors who say they can be fair, Jim told me. Few people will stand up in the courtroom and announce they're a bigot or a cop hater. If they do, they're hoping to get excused from jury duty. If a juror holds a bias or prejudice, they keep it to themselves. What is true about jury selection and people in general is that we keep our hateful side hidden from the outside world. I quickly learned to look for jurors whose life experience had colored their judgment and perception of people in a way that favored my client, whether a policeman, a patient, or a doctor. Jim told me that regardless of what a juror promised during jury selection, their life experience filtered what they heard and what they saw, affecting their thinking more than the evidence itself. I assumed that once jurors looked me in the eye and said they would be fair and impartial, they would do so in jury deliberations and rise above their personal biases. Jim said sometimes yes, but don't count on it. It took years for me to appreciate the reality of the courtroom; that the baggage of an individual's life experience, specifically political and religious values, reconstructs evidence to fit their preexisting beliefs. Jurors have a tendency to believe witnesses who appear to align with their views of the world.

Jury consultants help lawyers find the right jurors for a specific case, meaning individuals who walk into the jury box with a similar value system. For example, if you were the lawyer defending O. J. Simpson in his murder case, and your defense was that police planted damning evidence linking him (a popular black athlete) to the murder of his ex-wife and her friend, all of this set against the backdrop of riot-torn Los Angeles, with perpetual evidence of the police brutalizing black citizens, would you want 12 white businessmen and women and educated housewives from an upscale Los Angeles community, or eight black jurors and one Hispanic juror? The latter was the makeup of the O. J. Simpson criminal jury. More than a juror's education level and employment in the workforce, life experience shapes jurors' perception of evidence.

The more education a juror has, the better chance they will put aside personal bias and try to be fair. Regardless of how I viewed a not guilty verdict that did not make any sense to me given the evidence, post-verdict discussions revealed that the jurors thought they were fair and did the right thing.

The concept "know your audience" is not new. Jury selection, the inquiry of potential jurors, has little to do with jurors being fair; rather, it's finding people receptive to the facts of your case. The best example I've read on searching for receptive jurors comes from Trial Science, a national jury consultant group: "When Johnny Cash sang . . . I shot a man in Reno just to watch him die, at a concert inside Folsom Prison, the audience went wild." The prison guards, not so much. How would that song play out at a PTA meeting?

4 The Oath: An Exercise in Futility

Lesson 4: Righteous indignation and sarcasm have little persuasive value in the courtroom.

Every witness called to testify in court raises their right hand and answers this question: "Do you solemnly swear to tell the truth and nothing but the truth, so help you God?" In my experience, an honest response would be, "HELL NO."

The police had traced a stolen TV and stereo equipment found in the defendant's car to a burglary at an appliance store down the street from the apartment of the defendant's mother. The defendant's car was seen at the crime scene by a night watchman in the building next door. The defendant's lawyer wanted to plead his young client, Benny Carson, to receiving stolen property, a lesser offense with no jail time. "No way," I said in my customary dismissive tone. "Plead to a felony or go to trial." This exchange was typical of me in my three-year stint as a prosecutor. The cops and the prosecutor's office loved me. The defense bar despised me, and I would hear through my former classmates that the word on the street was "you're an unreasonable asshole." Looking back, I admit that I was flush with my role of chasing bad guys, and I was too indifferent to young defendants who didn't deserve jail time or a criminal record that could not be expunged. I should have been more considerate when hanging a felony on a young person.

A mistake made more frequently than others, because it occurs during the most stressful part of a trial, is cross-examination of witnesses. It's a time when intestines constrict to the size of a straw and the mental processor in the brain goes tilt. In my naïve state of mind, I believed that a witness would ultimately tell the truth because they were in a courtroom, under oath, in front of a judge. When the naïve lawyer hears an obvious untruth, they believe if they display obvious skepticism and become indignant, the jury will get the message and reject the witness's testimony. For example, a lawyer might raise their voice and say in a mocking tone, while looking at the jury, "So you want this jury to believe that you and the defendant were in your car driving to a movie theater ten miles away at the time victim was robbed?" An ineffective persuasion technique, unless a juror already feels that way.

A watertight alibi is a scarce commodity for criminal defendants. Alibi witnesses, often a friend or relative of the defendant, must present a credible scenario that "you got the wrong guy." They just can't say, "The clock tower struck ten just as we left the bar; we were long gone by the time the bartender was shot."

During my early years as a trial lawyer, I listened to audiotapes of Irving Younger on trial practice. Mr. Younger, a prolific and renowned lecturer on techniques of cross-examination, told his audience (as I remember it) that you can count on one hand the number of trial lawyers who possess the natural instincts to destroy a witness on cross-examination. "Don't fool yourself into thinking you are one of them," Younger said decisively. "The rest of us have to train our minds and master the skills of effective cross-examination," he added. As I mentioned previously, I had visited an Evidence class taught by Younger at Columbia Law School. I was on my way to backpack through Europe and I spent a couple of days with my high school friend Ed Fagan in New York City. He was a law student at Columbia, and he invited me to go with him to his Evidence class. (To this day, he takes credit for my Ivy League education.)

I've listened to Younger's "ten commandments of cross-examination" many times, especially Rule 6: Disallow Witness Explanation. Only Moses's Ten Commandments are broken more often.

Persuasive alibi witnesses usually time their involvement to an event occurring exactly at the time of the criminal act. For example, being someplace with the defendant while engaged in a normal social activity, like watching a TV show at the same time the robbery "went down."

The defense attorney called Benny's mother to the witness stand. *Easy pickings*, I thought. She walked timidly to the witness stand and smiled warmly at the jury. She was past middle age, wore her best church clothes, from what I could tell, and made her living cleaning other people's homes. The defense lawyer asked her to talk about her son and where he was on Friday night, the night of the burglary near her apartment building. She looked toward the jury and spoke softly. Her son, she said, was with her that night, watching her favorite TV show, *Happy Days*.

"Yeah, right," I said to myself. I expected the jury to see through her fabricated testimony. I was thinking this would be my Perry Mason moment. Cross-examination, as best I recall, went something like this:

Q. Now Mrs. Carson, you say you were home on the evening of Friday, January 10th?

A. Yes . . . yes, I was.

Q. Your son Benny owns a car, doesn't he?

A. Yes.

Q. And he drove over to your apartment Friday night, January 10th?

A. Why, no, he didn't. He took the city bus that stops a block from my apartment building. He had lent his car to a friend that evening.

Q. You told the jury Benny comes over most Friday evenings, correct?

A. Yes, he brings over his laundry and we spend the evening together.

Q. You testified that on Friday nights you and Benny like to watch *Happy Days*?

A. Yes, *Happy Days* comes on at eight o'clock. As I said before, I run the washer and dryer while we watch the show. Benny says Fonzie is the coolest.

Q. And you said, this Friday night, Benny rode the bus and brought his laundry over, right?

A. Why, yes, because I remember he didn't have his car.

Q. And you are telling the jury that you and Benny watched *Happy Days* together that night? (The tone of my voice rising incredulously with every question.)

A. Yes, we did.

Q. (Now each word rising to high indignation.) So Mrs. Carson, you want the jury . . . to believe . . . on January 10th . . . at around 8:00 p.m., the exact time of the burglary . . . three blocks from your house . . . that your son . . . was watching TV with you?

A. Yes he was, and that's the truth. (She turns her body to look directly at the jury.)

Only the greenest of trial lawyers would then say, "Mrs. Carson, can you look the judge in the eye and tell the same story?" I at least knew better than to make that mistake. In the courtroom a week before, in a case tried to a judge without a jury, a middle-aged woman bought a stolen washer and dryer with an original price tag of $500 for the tidy sum of $100, from a "friend of a friend." I asked her if she could look the judge in the eye and tell the truth. She made eye contact with the judge and said she had no idea the washer and dryer were stolen. "NOT GUILTY," ruled the judge.

Indignation, a common reaction to people who spew BS, has very little persuasive value in the courtroom, and is no substitute for hard facts. I am always surprised when I talk to jurors after an unfavorable verdict by their failure to share my disdain for witnesses that stretch the facts or who are in the business of testifying. The jury's lack of sensitivity is due to their lack of experience—meaning they don't hear similar versions of alibis week after week. They may be hard to believe, but they may be the only defense available. I still get indignant; I don't know a lawyer that can hold back when they hear a witness make stuff up on the witness stand. But there is a line that lawyers can't cross in the courtroom. When umbrage becomes sarcasm, jurors are offended. I can recall a jury commenting to both sides after a verdict that they "expected the lawyers to be passionate for their clients," but they didn't like the sarcastic comments my adversaries made during cross-examination of my witnesses. Criticism of an opponent or witness's credibility is best served by showing contradictions in words and deeds.

Contradictory evidence is a major technique used by lawyers to impeach a witness. There is a story often told about a backwoods trial lawyer in the 1800s that captures the essence of discrediting the believability of a witness. The murder charge against his client stemmed from an alcohol-fueled altercation. "Armstrong," a rowdy young man, used a homemade "slungshot" —a piece of lead tethered to a leather strap—striking Mr. Duff on the head. Duff died three days later. At trial, the chief prosecution witness said he saw the whole thing, though the fight occurred near midnight. On cross-examination, the roughhewn lawyer asked the eyewitness how he could be so sure he saw Armstrong hit Duff with a slungshot. There was a full moon out, he said, and added that he clearly saw Armstrong swing his slungshot and hit Duff in the head. The backwoods lawyer pulled out the Old Farmer's Almanac that showed the moon had already set at the time of the altercation. Reportedly, "the courtroom erupted in laughter." That backwoods lawyer was Abraham Lincoln.

Because our memory of events can be spotty and we make assumptions when our recall is faulty, the window of opportunity for impeachment is often ajar. Surely, impeachment techniques were used long before the days of Abraham Lincoln the trial lawyer, but human nature laughs at liars.

5 One Question Too Many

Lesson 5: Driving nails in a coffin is a dangerous practice on cross examination.

There are two stages in the development of a highly competent trial lawyer. The first stage is learning and developing trial skills. The second stage is the exercise of good judgment in the combative courtroom environment, under stress, in front of a hostile judge, emotions hermetically sealed and game face on while performing at a high level—a steep learning curve for even the most committed aspiring trial lawyer. *Knowing when to shut up* is both a skill and discipline. I have yet to reach the top of the curve.

A war story told at a seminar on cross-examination many years ago about the legendary Washington D.C. trial lawyer Edward Bennett Williams, in the early years of his career, paints a picture of the symbolic spear in the chest of a lawyer in love with the sound of his own voice. In the decades since, other celebrated lawyers have been substituted for Mr. Williams. One question too many has victimized most lawyers on many occasions. It's a skill I wish I used more often inside and outside the courtroom. Many things should go unsaid.

As the story goes, the prosecution witness, standing at the end of a dimly lit side alley, testified he saw two people fighting; the witness said that the defendant bit the ear off the victim. Mr. Williams, skilled at extracting concessions from witnesses on cross-examination that supported his client's innocence, began by asking precise questions that called for only "yes" or "no" answers:

Q. Your driver's license requires you to wear glasses when you drive a car, true?

A. Yes.

Q. You weren't wearing your glasses the night you saw two people struggling in the alley off 52nd Street, isn't that true?

A. No, I wasn't.

Q. Streetlights were on before you entered the alley, true?

A. Yes sir.

Q. Isn't it true, there were no streetlights illuminating the alley where you saw two men fighting?

A. Yes, sir.

Q. And, you told the police that it "was kinda dark at the time," true?

A. Yes.

Q. You told the police you were about 50 feet away when you heard men yelling, right?

A. Yes.

Q. You say you saw my client arguing with Mr. Jones, but you didn't see any blows exchanged, did you?

A. No sir.

Q. Mr. Jones claims the defendant bit him in the ear, but you didn't see my client bite Mr. Jones, isn't that true?

A. Well no, I didn't see him bite Mr. Jones.

At this moment Mr. Williams' tone deepens and his voice rises to make his point to the jury.

Q. So you can't tell the jury with any certainty that my client bit Mr. Jones, can you?

A. Yes . . . yes, I can. When he ran past me, I saw him spit out part of an ear.

Oops.

Overconfidence on cross-examination, and the desire to tie off the damaging testimony of an adverse witness and leave no lingering question in the jury's mind, can lead to courtroom catastrophes. After that fateful extra question, many a trial lawyer slinks back to counsel table with a large spear in the center of their chest. I'm humbled by the number of times I haven't learned this lesson.

The problem, however, is more than lack of experience or overconfidence. Some lawyers, mostly men, as my wife often reminds me, are enamored by the sound of their own voice. We think we're smarter than everyone else. We talk too much about ourselves and our opinions are so important we feel the need to share them with anyone that will listen. When it comes to persuasion, the axiom "less is more" applies, no matter how smart you think you are.

6 An Introduction to the Unpredictability of Pure Evil

Lesson 6: When it comes to personal safety, no one is immune from the dark side of the human condition.

I can still see that eight-by-ten glossy black-and-white morgue photograph of a beautiful young woman lying on her back: nude, glassy-eyed, staring at the ceiling. The cruel clarity of a large steak knife plunged between her breasts shocked me. Crime scene photographs have a surreal effect. They take you back to the repulsive moment of the end of a life—the pain and horror that convulsed the victim before the moment light turned to darkness.

One morning in Jim's office, looking for an assignment, I'd asked to see what case he was working on. He pointed to a large brown cardboard box next to his desk. I opened a folder marked "crime scene photos."

I saw for the first time a vile and terrifying ending to a young woman's life that was neither deserved nor expected. I had never seen evil in its purest form. I couldn't take my eyes away from the picture of the woman, her faced wiped of any expression, the handle of a butcher knife sticking out of her chest. Crime scenes of vicious murders suspend belief in humanity. I remember thinking that the guy that did this should fry in the electric chair. Part of the baggage carried by criminal lawyers for life are crime scene photos of horrific acts that are permanent reminders of the capacity for inhumanity that seethes in the mind of some people.

The woman in the photograph was Mrs. Mitchell. Jim O'Grady's colleague and the chief of the criminal division, Michael Miller, and his wife lived in the same apartment building and played bridge with the Mitchells on weekends. On the day of the murder, Mr. Mitchell came home from work and found the door locked. He pounded on the door, but his wife didn't answer. Her car was in the carport. *Something is not right*, he thought. Mr. Mitchell ran over to Mike's apartment and breathlessly told Mike, "Something is wrong." Mike had been an FBI agent before going to law school. And for some unexplainable reason, as he would say later, he stuck his revolver in his pants pocket.

It took both men to break open the door. They found Mrs. Mitchell in the upstairs bedroom, tied spread-eagle to the bed. Mr. Mitchell frantically searched for his infant son; the baby's crib was empty.

"I can't find the baby," he yelled to Mike, running downstairs. Mike found the three-month-old baby headfirst in the upstairs toilet. For three years the Mitchell murders went unsolved, until a prisoner told a guard in the Lucasville penitentiary that he would trade information about a murder rather than get transferred to another cell.

Once a sensationalized murder hits the newspapers, people suffering from some level of mental problems may call the police and confess to a murder they didn't commit. To sort through this bizarre behavior, police hold back certain details of a crime scene that only the killer would know.

Columbus police detectives interviewed John White at the maximum-security Southern Ohio Correctional Facility in Lucasville, Ohio, about an hour south of Columbus. White was serving time for armed robbery and assault. He repeated details about the Mitchell murder previously reported in the Columbus newspapers. The detectives were losing interest until he mentioned he'd found a small Kodak camera in a desk drawer. When he'd lifted the camera from the drawer, the camera clicked.

White told the detectives he had locked the door when he left Mitchell's apartment. He dropped the apartment key in razor slot in the old house where he lived in with his parents (a razor-disposal slot behind the sink was a common feature in bathrooms of old homes; the used razor blades dropped behind the wall of the bathroom). The detectives called Mr. Mitchell. He confirmed that one of the pictures later developed from the camera had what he thought at the time was an accidental view of the ceiling.

Armed with a search warrant for John White's parents' home, the police tore up the inside walls in the basement. Among rusty razor blades they found a house key, later matched to Mitchell's apartment. The jury convicted White of first-degree murder.

Years later, Mike visited John White in prison. The image of Mrs. Mitchell seared in his memory and the bedeviling question left unanswered, Mike asked White why he killed Mrs. Mitchell.

He didn't want any witnesses, White said.

That didn't surprise Mike, but he asked, "Why did you kill a three-month-old baby?" White just hung his head.

One dimension of criminal trial work is the immersion into dehumanizing behavior. It was in the prosecutor's office where I became acquainted with violence that some people are capable of. My takeaway from the prosecutor's office is that lying, cheating, stealing, bias, prejudice, infidelity, hatred, and violence are elements of the human condition. Every trial lawyer should be cognizant of the flaws in human behavior both inside and outside the courtroom.

7 Scarlet Letters

Lesson 7: Expect your opponent to exploit any real or perceived weaknesses in your evidence and witnesses.

Tactics and strategy are as important for trial lawyers as are the facts in the case—sometimes more so. Fear is a highly effective weapon that has been around since Moses came down from the mountain; not physical acts of cruelty, mind you, but bloodless psychological blows to the human psyche, otherwise known as intimidation. Trial lawyers plumb the depths of human weakness, looking to exploit every flaw, every failing, and every frailty—real or not—that may compromise their adversaries. Does the witness have something to hide? Maybe a single mother has two children by different fathers, or a doctor has failed to pass his or her board certification, or more recently, someone was involved in an episode of domestic violence or something stupid displayed on social media. As history unfolds and social mores change, the tactics remain the same. The prospect of embarrassment on the witness stand can be worse than the indiscretion itself.

The year was 1976. By now, after a full year in the trenches of courtroom combat, I had my sea legs. I picked up Mark McElwain's case from another prosecutor a few days before it was set for trial. This was not unusual for me. I wanted to be in trial every day, and I brought every ounce of intensity I possessed into the courtroom.

Mark supervised 40 employees at a local utility company. The defendant, one of the company's employees and an acquaintance of Mark, stole three checks from the top drawer of Mark's bedroom dresser. The defendant cashed the checks. He claimed through his lawyer that his friend Mark had given him the checks for personal reasons. The defendant, in his 20s, had a previous felony bad check charge reduced to a slap on the wrist. His lawyer demanded that I dismiss the charge. "What's the big deal? It was a misunderstanding."

I didn't care. I didn't say out loud "stick your head where the sun don't shine," but he got the message. To me, this was an open-and-shut case.

The prosecutor's office mailed subpoenas to witnesses three weeks before the trial. But, in minor felony cases like this one, I usually met the prosecuting witness, the victim, for the first time during the lunch break after selecting the jury. When I reviewed the file the weekend before the trial, I found a note written by one of our secretaries saying that the victim had called, wanting to know if it was necessary that he come to court. I called the contact number and spoke with Mark over the phone. Mark seemed reluctant. "It's OK with me if you reduce the charges," he said weakly. He tried to explain that his responsibilities at work demanded his full attention, and he didn't think he could take the day off on the day of the trial.

I figured since he knew the defendant, he felt bad that the guy could go to jail.

"It's necessary you be here," I told him. "You are under a subpoena." This was a veiled threat I relied on to encourage resistant witnesses to show up for trial. If there was no prosecuting witness the morning of trial, and if the judge refused to continue the trial date, I had to dismiss the case.

I met with Mark over the lunch break the first day of trial. I told him his testimony would be straightforward. I'd ask about his education, his job responsibilities, and if he knew the defendant from work. I reminded him of his statement to the police detective and not to forget the most important part of his testimony: "You did not give any checks to the defendant or authorize him to sign your name or withdraw money from your checking account." He understood.

Once both sides completed opening statements, Mark was my first witness. He appeared to be in his mid-40s. He was on the thin side and smartly dressed. He wore a knee-length, off-white, single-button trench coat, buttoned up to the second-to-last button. His coat collar was neatly turned down, displaying a perfectly knotted Windsor tie. His sandy blond hair was neatly coifed.

It was February. The need to wear an overcoat in the courtroom, which was at room temperature, seemed peculiar to me. Despite Mark's anxious body language and the judge reminding him to keep his voice up, I marched him through the elements of the check fraud case without a hiccup. Mark never looked in the direction of the defendant. Witnesses for the prosecution rarely do, unless a courtroom ID is required.

When the defense attorney rose to cross-examine, Mark's body stiffened, pressing his shoulders against the back of the witness chair. His jaw clenched. His body language displayed a distress signal to even the most casual observer. He gave the appearance of someone staring down the barrel of a 20-gauge shotgun. *What's this?* I wondered, as my stomach started to tighten—to this day I have never overcome the anxiety of sitting at counsel table watching my client or a critical witness fall apart on the witness stand.

Defense counsel began his cross-examination in a disdainful tone. He zeroed in on Mark's relationship with other office employees. At first, Mark's responses were measured. He seemed to be searching for answers to routine questions. Then defense counsel went staccato:

> You have drinks with a couple of employees after work, don't you?
>
> You've met Bobby here (pointing toward the defendant) many times after work, haven't you?
>
> Just you and him sharing drinks, right?

I objected. Multiple questions at one time were argumentative, not cross-examination.

Mark shifted back and forth in the witness chair with each question, almost like he was expecting a smack across the face. When defense counsel asked Mark to tell the jury about his boyfriend, I rose from my chair and shouted my objection, but it was too late. Blood began dripping from Mark's nose. He tipped his head back, cupping his hand under his chin. The court reporter, always ready to hand a sobbing witness a box of facial tissues, rushed to the witness stand. The judge granted my request for a short recess. I escorted Mark to an anteroom—a small witness meeting room adjacent to the courtroom.

Mark slumped into a chair, pale and short of breath. "Do I have to go back out there?" he asked, putting both hands to his face.

"Yes, you do," I said.

He questioned why we just couldn't let the defendant plead guilty.

"We can't," I said. "It's too late for that."

It wasn't too late to offer a plea, but I was pissed at defense counsel. This trial was about him and me now. Why was the defense lawyer beating up Mark when there was no question that the checks were stolen? Well, I understood very quickly. Back in the 70s, who on the jury would believe a "homo," as gay men were often derisively called? I am not proud to confess I said those things, too.

Mark sidled up to the witness stand like he had large pebbles in his shoes, bright-red blood smudged on the lapel of his trench coat.

The court sustained my objection, there being no probative value between Mark's boyfriends and the defendant forging checks. The judge limited cross-examination to Mark's relationship with the defendant and reminded Mark he was still under oath. Defense counsel had banked on Mark refusing to show up and testify for fear of getting outed in the courtroom, forcing me to drop the charges. The only defense tactic left was insinuating Mark and the defendant were lovey-dovey—that Mark didn't mind missing a few checks—no real loss here, ladies and gentlemen of the jury.

What seemed like a paint-by-the-numbers two-to-three-day trial turned into character assassination—nothing to do with the merits of the charges. Yet the insinuating questions and the droplets of blood smeared on the lapel of Mark's London Fog sent the message to the jury: Mark was gay and not worthy of belief. I could barely control my anger, watching the defense lawyer use shame and embarrassment to discredit an otherwise truthful witness. This was a new experience for me. It was a feeling of helplessness. I couldn't stop the decapitation of my witness. I've learned that the best I can do is anticipate the blows to come and prepare the witness to deflect the weaknesses in their testimony or provide a reasonable explanation.

I was angry all the time when I was a prosecutor. I didn't know it then, but my aggressive, competitive personality made me a good fit for the courtroom. Many times during trial, I wanted to punch the defense lawyer in the face. My overt aggressiveness would become a problem for me when I spoke the language of a plaintiff's lawyer, asking jurors for money in civil cases.

In my early stages of trial work, it was not beyond me to make disparaging comments to my opponent, especially to a lawyer I didn't like, and in my early years, I was too self-centered to compliment defense lawyers after I'd won at trial. Many defense lawyers I faced were sharp in the courtroom, but criminal cases with three eyewitnesses pointing their finger at the defendant in the courtroom are near impossible for defense lawyers to win.

After the jury found the defendant guilty of check fraud, instead of being gracious with the usual perfunctory handshake most lawyers proffer, win or lose, I walked up to defense counsel and said, "You're a jerk."

Instead of firing back an equivalent insult, he held out his hand. "I've got a responsibility to my client," he said impassively.

The defense counsel's strategy targeted the witness's background, not the truth of what was said—the tried-and-true tactic of destroying a witness's believability. If the jury found Mark's personal behavior distasteful, they would be less likely to believe his testimony.

I had a long climb to the top of the learning curve of the subtleties of jury trials, but I learned quickly to expect defense counsel to expose any generally recognized personal dalliance of my witness in the courtroom. Making a witness unworthy of the jury's respect damages more than their likeability—it destroys credibility.

It took me a while to get used to defense lawyers fighting to exonerate their client when the evidence of guilt, in my mind, far outweighed any evidence of innocence. Defense counsel, I realized, would try to create doubt by finding a tiny seed of truth to support a theory, nourishing the seedling, giving it water and sunlight, and growing it into a blooming reality that cast a shadow of doubt on the deliberative mind of the jury. Is this justice? If you're the lawyer defending the accused, it certainly is.

It would take many years for me to accept the meaning of justice as defined by trial lawyers, not the books and articles published by well-meaning justices on the Supreme Court, nor the all-knowing media pundits calling for justice, pushing for prosecution and conviction. Trial work is a fiercely competitive environment. Highly skilled trial lawyers perform at a high level, just like professional athletes, except their mental performance and focus may have to last for weeks, not a single afternoon. By now, the legendary coach Vince Lombardi's mantra *"winning is the only thing"* is a cliché. Yet once a trial lawyer steps in the courtroom, only winners get justice. Prosecutors must prove their case *beyond a reasonable doubt*. A not-guilty verdict because of insufficient evidence to persuade a jury of the defendant's guilt *beyond a reasonable doubt* is justice, despite my view of the damning evidence.

Again, O. J. Simpson comes to mind. A not-guilty verdict does not mean the defendant was innocent. However, it does mean the defendant's lawyers proved the prosecutor's evidence was too weak to convince a jury beyond a reasonable doubt. It's justice, whether I like it or not.

8 Inside the Basement of Medical Knowledge

Lesson 8: Don't watch an autopsy.

One Saturday morning, my phone rang at 7:30 a.m. I had one phone in my apartment, a wall phone in the kitchen. I didn't get up, even though the caller let it ring forever. Then, minutes later, the phone rang again. Saturday mornings usually found me semi-conscious. Friday night, I might not get home until late or not at all. I'd get up by noon, mosey down to the office, prepare my cases for the coming week, and entertain the married guys with exaggerations and half-truths about the night before.

"There's been a murder, and two children are missing," the detective said when I finally answered. "You need to go down to the morgue."

"Can't someone from the crime scene unit do this?" I asked, half perturbed.

"No," he said, "I don't want any issues with *chain of custody*."

I knew defense lawyers sometimes tried to exclude crime scene evidence if there was a break in the custodial chain of evidence from the scene of the crime to the courtroom—the argument being that the evidence had been tampered with. When I hung up the phone, I thought, *OK, this must be an important case.*

I wasn't enthused about the sight of a dead body. I remember reading in high school how medical students in the 18th and 19th centuries relied on body snatchers to dig up bodies for dissection. But the only thing I was there for was a couple of bullets. This can't be that bad, I thought; I could stand in a corner somewhere.

In the 1970s, pathologists at Ohio State University College of Medicine handled coroners' cases. The elected coroner was a family-practice physician. The actual autopsies were supervised by two or three OSU pathologists sworn in as deputy coroners, with most of the actual dissections done by medical residents under faculty supervision. Here, there was not much mystery on the cause of death given the couple of extra holes in the victim's head.

I remember that Saturday morning, because it changed the trajectory of my career.

Two cops were waiting for me. They sat in the first row of aluminum bleachers used by medical students and doctors-in-training to observe autopsies. One of the two policeman asked, "Are you Todaro?"

One of the officers lifted a donut from a brown paper lunch bag. "Jelly donut?" he asked, raising the donut to eye level.

At the head of the table was a small stainless steel basin for rinsing off blood from organs and body parts. More shiny stainless steel wash basins and cabinets framed one side of the room. The walls were yellow-glazed bricks that had long ago lost their luster. This place had the feel of an old black-and-white Frankenstein movie—and why was there a large drain in the middle of the gray cement floor? Later I'd see the entire room, basins, table, and anything stainless steel, hosed down, blood-tinged water swirling down the drain.

"Hey, you need to change into scrubs and get booties for your shoes. Follow me," yelled an assistant. Later I would learn he was called a Deaner—a morgue worker responsible for handling bodies once delivered to the morgue. I didn't say yes, and I didn't say no; I just followed this guy dressed in powder blue cotton pajamas to a cave-like room to change. The room was cold. This was so abnormal, so strange, that I wanted to leave.

I watched as photographs of the body were taken. The body was rolled on its side to photograph the back. I knew that autopsy photos were used to identify evidence of bruises or cuts on the victim's arms and back that could show the victim tried to defend against an attack, or that a photograph of multiple stab wounds in the victim's back might convince a jury that the defendant hadn't acted in self-defense.

"We're ready," the young doctor-in-training shouted, looking in my direction. I walked up to the dissection table, trying to act like it was just another day. Yeah, I've stood over naked bodies before, blood caked below their noses, doll's eyes the opacity of marbles, fixed on the ceiling. I don't know why, but I was utterly fascinated. The young doctor raised a scalpel to the guy's neck and cold-bloodedly cut a straight line from the sternal notch—the dip above where the two collarbones meet in the center of the chest—down to his belly button. She used an autopsy bone saw to cut through the center of his rib cage, then spread his chest, like a canoe, exposing his lungs. Next, she cut through the muscles of the abdomen and dissected down to the liver and intestines. At the sight of the guy's guts, I stepped back over by the cops. *Oh no, I don't want to throw up in front of the cops.*

I walked back to the table. The doctor had cut open the small intestine, and the putrid stench of decomposing bacteria escaped, wafting over the body and me. One whiff drove me behind the bleachers, my stomach knocking at my tonsils. The young doctor seemed unfazed by the smell. During the dissection, the resident was describing what she saw. Cigarette smoking caused his lungs to appear grayish. His coronary arteries had narrowed because of atherosclerotic disease. I was told there was a benign cyst on his liver.

Deputy coroner Nobuhisa Baba, MD, PhD, one of the university pathologists, had just entered the morgue. The PhD after a doctor's name means that they have a doctorate degree on top of a doctor degree and not only treat patients, but engage in medical research. These doctors are at the high end of an already very high academic curve. Dr. Baba took over the dissection. As the deputy coroner, he oversaw autopsies in homicide cases.

The death was an obvious homicide. The victim had two small holes in the back of his head, but no exit wounds. The only issue in the death of this victim was finding the bullets. I was supposed to take possession of them and deliver them to forensics, which would attempt to match the bullets with the handgun used in the murder, if it was found, and then trace the weapon to the defendant.

Dear reader, if it was hard to stomach reading about the dissection above, you should consider skipping the next two paragraphs. I'm sorry.

To preserve the option of an open-casket funeral, post-mortem examination of the head requires the incision to start behind the ear above the hairline, and extend over the top of the head and cross over to the opposite ear. The front half of the scalp is pulled forward over the face and the back half of the scalp pulled toward the back of the head, exposing the glistening, bony white skull. Using a special circular bone saw, the doctor saws 360 degrees around the exposed skull, and the top half (skull cap) is removed. The brain is severed from the spinal cord and removed. Then the skull cap is put back in its original position and the scalp sewed together and the sutures hidden within the hairline, leaving no one the wiser at the funeral service.

It was the thought of breathing in bone dust that sickened me for the third time. I don't recall anyone wearing a surgical mask. I tried to hold my breath, then I tried to take shallow breaths, but I had to walk away. My face must have had a bluish tinge, or maybe no color at all.

"Are you OK?" one of the cops asked, smiling.

Dr. Baba motioned me back to the table. He was tracking the bullet holes through the remnants of the victim's brain. Both bullets had passed through the brain and lodged inside the skull, opposite the entry points, but lower.

I asked Dr. Baba, "Did the path of the bullet mean the shooter stood above the man when he fired?"

"Both bullets entered the skull in a downward path," he said, using hand movements to illustrate direction. "The victim could have been kneeling or lying down when he was shot, I can't tell you any more than that." Baba asked the resident if she'd seen powder burns around the entry sites. When a gun is fired at close range—approximately a foot or so—black gunpowder residue may show up on the victim's skin.

The resident said she had checked for powder on the man's scalp before she removed the skull cap. "No residue," she said.

I later learned the defendant didn't take too kindly to the victim having an affair with his estranged wife. The defendant had broken into the victim's home and shot him in the living room. He muffled the shots from his handgun by firing through a couch cushion pressed against the victim's head. At the scene, police found two bullet holes in the cushion, ringed by gunpowder.

There's no Hallmark ending to an autopsy. The flattened small-caliber bullets retrieved from inside the skull were rinsed and placed in a small plastic bag marked with the victim's name and autopsy number. All incisions were sutured with morgue twine. Later, morticians would use better sutures, and all evidence of the autopsy would be hidden from view.

I asked the police officers what I should do with the evidence.

"I'll take those," the lead donut cop offered, holding out his hand.

"Hey," I said, pulling the evidence back from his reach, "Ron wanted me down here to take custody of the bullets and get them to the crime lab for testing."

"We'll take them," he said, then boomed with laughter. In unison both said, "Welcome to homicide, Todaro!"

Months later, I couldn't get the autopsy out of my head. My autopsy experience reminded me of watching episodes of *The Twilight Zone*.

9 A Cadaver Named Otis

Lesson 9: Knowledge of anatomy and physiology are a malpractice lawyer's stock in trade.

Months later, I stood next to Dr. Baba, watching an autopsy of another homicide victim. Dr. Baba had grown up in Japan during World War II. He'd spent many nights in the subways of Tokyo, one of the few places he found enough light to study. Dr. Baba was brilliant, but spoke horrible English.

I was fascinated by forensic pathology. I asked Dr. Baba if I could take a course from him at the medical school. He said yes, but first I had to learn anatomy and get at least some introduction to histology, the microscopic examination of human tissue.

Pathologists can look at unidentified human tissue under a microscope and recognize the cell's origin. Liver tissue looks entirely different than kidney tissue. Heart muscle cells look entirely different than muscle cells in the leg. I asked Dr. Baba where I could buy a textbook on anatomy so I could start the education process.

"No books," he said. "You must go to cadaver lab." He told me to talk with an anatomy professor by the name of Peggy Hines. She taught anatomy to first-year medical students.

I met Margaret H. Hines in her office near the anatomy lab. She had served in the Women's Army Medical Specialist Corps as a physical therapist after WWII and had earned a PhD in anatomy at Ohio State. She was a large-framed woman. Her blonde hair had a yellowish tinge, and she wore red high-heeled shoes that made loud clicking sounds as she walked on the marble floors of the anatomy building. Months later, I was amused by the instant spark of energy in the custodians and lab attendants at the sound of high heels coming down the hallway. Dr. Hines was not afraid to speak her mind, and she was a force within the university.

Dr. Hines arranged for me to have my own cadaver as a continuing education student at Ohio State University. I named him Otis, after Jim Otis, All-American fullback at Ohio State. Dr. Hines supervised my dissection two days a week for the next six months.

The anatomy lab introduced me to the depth of knowledge about the complexity of the function of the human body, as well as the daunting demands on medical students. Initially, we all had to overcome the cadaver smell. Cadavers are pickled in formaldehyde, a preservation fluid that gives off a powerful odor that stings the eyeballs, infiltrates hair and clothing, and seeps under the cuticles of well-polished fingernails. It even tricks the mind. I smelled formaldehyde in my tuna fish sandwiches (my usual dinner) for weeks.

After six months of anatomy, I spent the next four months with Dr. Baba. Autopsies opened my eyes to the untidy world of medicine, especially the humbling challenge of diagnosis.

On the autopsy table one Saturday morning was a 17-year-old male who died in the hospital weeks after a kidney transplant. Despite constant attention and intervention to treat the wild fluctuations of his vital signs and lab data, doctors lost the battle. But they didn't know why.

Standing around the body when the autopsy began were the patient's surgeon, his urologist, his nephrologist, and a medical student. When Dr. Baba exposed the transplanted kidney, the surgeon yelled, "Where the hell did all these clots come from?" Even after Dr. Baba completed the dissection, the question remained unanswered. This was not the first or the last time after completion of an autopsy that physicians were left guessing about what caused a body's organs to fail.

My time with Dr. Baba brought me to the doorstep of the doctors' world of uncertainty—the daily confrontation of "unexplained presentation of symptoms." I didn't realize at the time the fertile ground for malpractice lawsuits this unpredictable and unknowable side of medicine would become in my legal practice. Doctors who are compelled to make decisions under time constraints based on incomplete data, with imprecise and shifting information, sometimes guess wrong. During those nine months at Ohio State, I learned doctors are vulnerable to *hindsight analysis*. Hindsight wipes away uncertainty and confusion, making the diagnosis as easy for jurors to see as a train chugging down the tracks. Yet making the diagnosis in real time is sometimes nearly impossible. Soon, I would master the technique of hindsight analysis—rubbernecking medical treatment in the rearview mirror.

Now as I look back, I see a quality in doctors that is seldom rewarded in the courtroom, but is so important to the daily practice of medicine. Doctors must possess a tolerance for uncertainty. They must embrace it when making life and death decisions. All of us make decisions when we lack the information necessary to know—for sure—we are doing the right thing. Imagine, though, being forced to make quick decisions with sketchy information every day, and if you're wrong, you end up in the courtroom—a large malpractice verdict invalidating your hard-earned reputation.

10 Fear Invisible to the Naked Eye

Lesson 10: Use buzzwords: find the word or sentence that captures the emotional essence of the factual bases of your case.

After drinking all evening with her girlfriend by her side, Carla left a singles bar at closing time, arm-in-arm with two guys who had bought her a couple of vodka tonics. She had told her girlfriend she had a ride home. Instead of driving her home, they stopped at another bar for a nightcap, and afterward, the two men drove to a desolate area of town. The detective's report of Carla's statement of what happened that night was less than reassuring. I was surprised the grand jury came down with an indictment.

I met Carla in the lobby of the prosecutor's office late on a Friday afternoon. She would have fit in at any college campus. She had long, dark hair, wore bell-bottom jeans frayed at the ends, and a skinny rib sweater.

In my office Carla stood behind the chair in front of my desk, clutching her beaded handbag. I remember asking, "Are you OK?" and saying, "We need to talk about what happened."

After a moment of staring through me, she sat down. I asked her to tell me what happened. Awkward silence seemed to last for minutes. So I asked Carla to tell me a little bit about herself, expecting to put her at ease and break her icy demeanor. "He forced me," she blurted, then more silence.

I knew she was uncomfortable, and frankly, so was I.

"Look," I said, "I'm on your side. I have to know everything about what happened that night."

I thought it might help if I told her I had experience in sexual assault cases and that I would do my best to help her get through this. I explained that we had to show the jury that she had no idea the events would unfold as they did.

After a long pause, her demeanor changed. Surprisingly, her voice was flat and devoid of the hurtful tone that would give her credibility in front of a jury. No weepy eyes, no trembling of her lower lip revealing the aftershock of a traumatic event. Within ten minutes of our meeting, I knew my problem was more than the facts. It's not that I didn't believe her, but would a jury believe her? I had learned from my jury experience that jurors evaluate truthfulness by how the witness comes across on the witness stand. The jury would expect to hear the pain in Carla's voice, to see tears and emotion. Once Carla controlled her emotions, she showed me nothing.

My initial interview technique followed the typical prosecutorial template: First, let the victims tell their story. Second, look for facts that don't add up and find the explanation as to why they don't. And third, ask the tough questions the defense lawyer will ask on cross-examination and make sure the victim's answers don't hurt the prosecution of the case. For me and Carla, the challenge was her credibility on the issue of consent.

I couldn't tell Carla she would make a shitty witness; my job was to coach her to be a more believable witness. But the bigger problem was her story.

"Facts are stubborn things," John Adams, trial lawyer and later president of the United States, once told a jury. I had this feeling rising in my gut that men on the jury would hear her story and scoff, "She asked for it." In our second meeting, I tried to prepare Carla for the attack on her credibility in the courtroom. I reminded her that the defense attorney would ask embarrassing questions and become indignant when she denied that sex on the hood of an MGB was not consensual. Instead of calling her a liar, I told her, he would raise his voice, his tone incredulous that anyone would believe her accusations.

"It will go like this," I said. "He'll say, 'So you're telling the jury, you were forced to jump on the hood of a car, roll over on your back and unzip your jeans, that's what you want this jury to believe?'"

But there was more, and this fact was something that not even a pubescent teenager would ignore. The police detective underlined one sentence in Carla's statement about what happened that night: "When the two men dropped me off at my apartment, I kissed the driver on the cheek."

My fellow prosecutors just shook their heads. "So, she kissed the guy on the cheek who raped her ten minutes earlier?"

At this second meeting, I had to revisit with Carla why she kissed the rapist. The defense lawyer would build his defense around her statement that she kissed the defendant after he drove her to her apartment. He would argue this was a sign of affection, not fear. Why didn't she jump out of the car and run to her apartment where it was safe?

She couldn't explain the moment she kissed the defendant on the cheek. I asked her a question which was technically a suggestion. "Maybe you were just too scared."

"He did hurt me," she said dispassionately. "He punched me."

I had forgotten that the police report had mentioned, "The victim said she was punched in the stomach." I got the sense she felt I was interrogating her. That I wasn't on her side. I stopped short of digging into more embarrassing details. I didn't want her to start crying. I'd never hear the end of it from women staffers.

I had another concern: Would Carla even show up to testify? When I asked if she was ready to come to court, she told me that after many late-night conversations with her girlfriends, she had summoned the courage to press charges.

"I'm not going to let *him* get away with this," she said as she left my office. Her closest friend would be with her.

"What about your parents?" I had asked.

"They live out of town. I haven't told them," she said, almost in a whisper.

I believed Carla, though I could not ignore the shadow of skepticism that darkened the enthusiasm of the investigating detective's report. However, Susan, a young married woman, newly hired in our fledgling, underfinanced Victim/Witness Program, thought differently. She told me that no young woman was going to come into this office and subject herself to the worst kind of shameful experience if it hadn't happened.

"She will be shamed whether this jerk is convicted or not," she said, appealing to my chivalrous side. If Susan believed Carla, I believed Carla. But would the jury believe Carla?

The week before the trial, the defendant's lawyer stopped by my office to chat. These conversations were typical and always congenial. Defense lawyers usually laid out the reasons why I should reduce the charges to justify a lenient sentence. Don Reuben, the defendant's lawyer, was both skilled and expensive. He wanted the rape charge dropped or reduced to simple assault, a misdemeanor, which later could be expunged from his preppy client's record.

I refused to bargain.

I didn't have a deeper understanding of the lasting effects of traumatized rape victims that would come much later in my career. In the 1970s, there was no one to explain how women fearful of being beaten or killed react to rape. Carla's case occurred years before research showed that women go into survival mode when physically overwhelmed by an attacker, instinctively pacifying, or reacting with oddly familiar behavior, believing and praying the attacker won't hurt or kill them. But her incomprehensible act of affection after being raped was a staggering blow to our case.

Of all the roadblocks to a rape conviction, none are more daunting than the lack of evidence of force. Carla reported the rape seven days after it happened. The detective's report mentioned there were no signs of trauma.

My only visual recall of Carla's tread to the witness stand is her pristine beige loose-fitting dress slacks and lack of makeup. Susan had suggested church clothes: no jeans, no heels, no beaded handbag, and no sunflower dress. At first Carla's voice fluttered, but she steadied herself after telling the jury she grew up in a one-stoplight town near Toledo, dropped out of Ohio State, and worked as a receptionist for a Columbus dentist.

I asked Carla to tell the jury what happened that night. She looked at me rather than at the jury, too nervous to follow my instructions to speak to the jurors. Witnesses must eyeball the jury, or they'll think the witness is hiding something. After about five seconds of unnerving silence, Carla said she and her girlfriend met two guys at a bar called The Yardarm. It was "drink and drown" night. Two young men bought them vodka tonics and made them laugh. Carla's friend, who was driving, wanted to leave because it was getting late. One of the guys offered to give Carla a ride back to her apartment. Carla told her girlfriend not to worry, she had a ride home. I asked her if the driver of the car was in the courtroom. After a half second glance, she pointed to the defendant.

She testified that she squeezed in between the bucket seats of a neat two-seater MG convertible. For any guy on the jury, the visual was Carla straddling the gearshift between her legs. She said they hit one more bar before heading to her apartment. Instead of driving her home, they drove to a desolate spot by abandoned railroad tracks. The driver pinned her to the hood of his MG while the other guy watched.

"When they dropped you off at your apartment, what happened next?"

"I kissed him."

"You mean the man that raped you? Why did you do that?" I asked, feigning a quizzical tone. I had mentioned the kiss in my opening statement to the jury, hoping to lessen the sting of the baffling human behavior that would be perceived as consent.

"I was in shock," she said, looking away from the jury. "I don't know why I did that."

I finished my direct examination and returned to the counsel table, waiting for the defense attorney to disembowel Carla.

Don Reuben was hell-on-wheels in the courtroom. He was tall, slender, with dark curly hair, and wore a navy blue suit every day in the courtroom. He wasted no time.

"A female police detective examined you at the police station after you claimed you were raped, right?"

"Yes, but . . . ." Don interrupted Carla's answer and fired another question.

"There wasn't a mark on you, was there?"

Carla's face suddenly hardened but her voice pleaded, "He broke my nose, that's what my doctor told me."

Don's face blanched. He objected immediately. I was surprised, too. The judge took a short recess. Don exploded as we walked into the judge's chambers. "What the doctor told her is inadmissible hearsay and Todaro ambushed me," he said, pointing a finger in my face. Don wanted a mistrial.

"How could Todaro not know she had a broken nose?" he shouted. "Todaro sucker-punched me, Your Honor. He hid evidence. How do I really know she had a broken nose, when it was broken, or what the doctor actually said?"

Most of the time trial lawyers become indignant to make a point, but Don was genuinely angry. The judge was annoyed, too. If he granted a mistrial, he would have to spend another week in the courtroom. He didn't grant a mistrial, but he ruled that Carla could only tell the jury the defendant punched her in the nose and she sought medical treatment two weeks after the incident. The judge then instructed the jury to disregard any conversations with any individuals other than the defendant. Too late. The jury had heard the damaging evidence, and as all lawyers know, it's humanly impossible to unring a bell.

The jury convicted the defendant. It didn't matter what I believed. It didn't matter what the defense lawyer told the jury. The jury believed a broken nose.

The verdict was another lesson in competency in trial work. I had ineptly cut short my prep session with Carla before digging into all the facts. Her doctor's visit occurred two weeks after the police report. I didn't thoroughly investigate the case and I didn't know all the facts because I was too fixated on one shiny object: kissing the rapist. That factual circumstance narrowed my focus and, consequently, my investigation. Of course, in the back of my mind, I see Scott wagging his finger: "Know the facts."

My coming-of-age moments during Carla's trial have lasted in memory these many years. We almost had a mistrial; we almost lost because I failed to know a critical fact; we almost lost because the victim's conduct didn't conform with the jurors' personal beliefs and expectations of how a woman should react when assaulted; and we almost lost because the witness's credibility was compromised by a cultural bias—a young woman putting herself in a position that welcomes danger deserves what she gets. Back then, a woman's poor judgment was a character flaw; not at all the same as a man's poor judgment chalked up to youth, or the attitude that "boys will be boys."

I was beginning to understand. There was more to winning than presenting the facts. Some facts have an explosive impact on a jury and can, as the lawyers say, turn a jury on a dime. But the lasting lesson, the power of buzzwords—a sentence or a word infused with emotion—changes minds quicker than a litany of facts. "He punched me and broke my nose" would have forced the defendant to plead guilty to a felony.

For example, in the case of the patient who died from uncontrollable bleeding during gallbladder surgery, "no one bleeds to death during a routine gallbladder procedure unless the doctor was negligent." Or in a case where the doctor failed to recognize obvious symptoms of a serious disease, "the symptoms of headache and blurred vision were red flags warning of a fatal stroke." One sentence can induce an emotional reaction overcoming compelling evidence. The lesson for me was to find a phrase that triggered an image or emotion in the jurors' minds that propelled the theory of my case.

11 The Business of a Contingent Fee Lawyer

Lesson 11: Society still sees advertising personal injury lawyers as ambulance chasers, until they need a lawyer to right a wrong.

After eight months, I prosecuted 33 jury and non-jury trials. I was super aggressive. I flamed out after three years and approximately 75 jury and non-jury felony trials, by my estimation. I joined a small personal injury firm as a minor partner, meaning I was responsible for 25 percent of the monthly expenses. I ran out of my savings in two months. The experience of indebtedness to friends and creditors in law school and having no ability to pay my bills was an agonizing experience never to be forgotten. I jumped ship.

Shafer & Higgins, one of the first boutique personal injury firms in Columbus, hired me after a thumbs-up from old-school criminal defense lawyers who had tried cases against me. My medical background helped. Harmon Shafer, the older of the two partners, gave me an advance so I could pay my rent. Dan Higgins was president-elect of what was then called the Ohio Academy of Trial Lawyers (now the Ohio Association for Justice), "the voice for plaintiff's trial lawyers in Ohio." Mr. Shafer had built a reputation as the leading medical malpractice lawyer in central Ohio. Mr. Higgins was a crafty, up-and-coming personal injury lawyer.

When I joined the firm, Dan Higgins had more than 500 personal injury cases in the office. Most were rear-end auto accident claims. Few went to trial, but the cases that did usually involved disputed liability: Who had the green light? Who failed to yield the right of way?

In many whiplash cases, damages were hotly contested. Insurance adjusters scoffed at demands for thousands of dollars in cases where an eggshell dent on the back bumper led to the client missing work for three months. Many of our clients expected tens of thousands of dollars, when the case was worth maybe a $750 after the medical expenses were paid. Clients may have heard or read about someone getting hundreds of thousands of dollars in a lawsuit. Getting our clients' astronomical expectations down to earth involved hours of face-to-face meetings.

A universal naïveté shared by injured clients is the unwavering faith that jurors will believe every word they say. Anger mounted and discussions became heated when I tried to explain that a jury might not believe their neck sprain took three months to heal. While counseling plaintiffs with unreasonable expectations, I have never mastered the diplomacy of telling a client, "Your lack of education, your whiny personality, and your sloppy appearance on the witness stand makes you a poor witness—you're neither believable nor sympathetic."

Advising clients that a jury could award less than the cost of going to trial, and recommending settling for a small sum a week before trial, usually ended bitterly, with the client snatching the pittance of a settlement check off my desk and muttering as they walked out of my office about how they got screwed by a shitty lawyer.

After six months working with Dan, I made the mistake of complaining about all these shitty cases. He was quick to enlighten me on the mantra of Shafer & Higgins.

"We make silk purses out of sows' ears," he said, annoyed by my failure to appreciate the lifeline of the firm. "We make a living from other lawyers' headaches."

"Jesus, Dan, juries won't like our clients. They look like they're trying to get something for nothing."

Dan shot me one of those *what the hell is wrong with you?* looks. "We take these shitty cases from referring lawyers so when a big damage case comes along, we get the big case."

Dan fought hard for his clients without judging their character, an essential trait of a veteran trial attorney. Dan and Mr. Shafer advocated for every client, young or old, even when they anticipated the case was a loser. They waited, hoping the referring lawyer would send them the bellringer.

What set Dan apart from the average plaintiff's lawyer was his commitment to the craft of trial work. Successful personal injury lawyers were both skilled in the courtroom and had the stomach to try difficult cases. Lawyers who tucked their tails between their legs and settled cheap lost the intimidation factor necessary to reap good settlements. On Monday mornings, after I spent the weekend preparing for a sore-back case, Dan liked to walk into my office, sit across from my desk, cross his legs man-style, sip his first cup of coffee, look up at the ceiling, and wonder aloud, "Is he an office tiger or a courtroom lamb?"

Yeah, I knew. *Don't settle cheap.*

***

By December, both partners were confident I had made the mental switch from prosecutor to plaintiff's lawyer. Two weeks before Christmas, Mr. Shafer plopped a slim file on the corner of my desk.

"There's a pretrial in this case at 1:30 p.m.," he said. "I want you to cover it."

"*No problemo,*" I said.

As Mr. Shafer walked out of my office, he looked over his shoulder and half-bellowed, "And don't take any shit!"

I never do, I said to myself. I had been one of the golden boys in the prosecutor's office, or at least I had thought so. I had knocked heads with some of the best criminal lawyers in central Ohio. I'd prosecuted high-profile murder cases. In three years, I had tried more jury trials than any lawyer *ever* in the same period of time in the prosecutor's office. When the office had started a victim-assistance division, I was one of the prosecutors they went to first—they liked the passion I brought to the courtroom. I had earned a reputation as one of the go-to trial lawyers in the prosecutor's office. I didn't take any crap from anyone . . . except my bosses, and a few judges who took exception to my so-called witness badgering and uncompromising plea deals that forced unnecessary trials.

I leafed through the file during lunch. The plaintiff, a young child, had lost two baby teeth after falling off Santa's lap at a shopping mall on the west side of town. Mr. Shafer, a fearless trial lawyer, sued the mall owner. I laughed when I saw the name of one of the defendants: "AKA Santa Claus." *Two baby teeth?* I chuckled. Mr. Shafer must have a nutty sense of humor. Unfortunately, the insurance adjuster for the mall owner was not amused. He denied the claim. When adjusters refused to settle, Shafer & Higgins immediately filed suit. There would be no whining or pleading for a small settlement. "Can't we just put a little money in the client's pocket, and we won't sue?" Not Shafer & Higgins; they never beg.

As I perused the file, newspaper clippings in an unsealed packet in the back pocket of the file caught my eye. *Wow*, I thought, *publicity, my kind of case*. The lawsuit had made its way to Johnny Carson's *Tonight Show*. In law school, one of my late-night study break pasttimes was watching Carson's monologue, then back to the books. The local newspapers had reported parts of Johnny's opening monologue on the Santa incident.

I can't remember the entirety of the blurb in the newspaper, but I remember the punch line. I can visualize Johnny's usual style for delivery of a funny punch line: "I just saw something in the news . . . a lawyer in Columbus, Ohio, sued Santa Claus." I imagined another pause, then the masterful trademark deadpan: "The lawyer is calling the tooth fairy as an expert witness."

The judge had set the pretrial for two weeks before Christmas—unusual since courthouse activity slowed at holiday time. Judges hold pretrials in a small-damage case like this one in the judge's chambers with only the lawyers from both sides present, no clients. The judge might ask how discovery is going, or if the case will be ready for trial. Eventually, the judge will ask about settlement—the real reason for pretrials. Settling a case on the judge's docket saves judges and their staff a lot of work.

The walk from our office to the courthouse took about ten minutes. The sky had turned gun-barrel gray, with a biting wind but no snow; a typical mid-December day in Columbus. I wore my beige double-breasted trench coat over one of my Brooks Brothers suits. Luckily, today was Friday. I wore my most lawyer-like suits on Friday. Not that I expected to go to court that day—happy hour Friday afternoon started when the clock struck five, and the circuit awaited. Lounge lizards wore chains around their necks, but young lawyers on tour after work wore their standard attire: charcoal gray suits, white shirts with the top button unfastened, and crimson neckties, casually loosened. That's what I wore, my tie not yet undone.

The lobby in the courthouse was empty. I punched the elevator button to the seventh floor. When the doors slid open, I saw a group of people gathered around the entrance to Judge Branson's courtroom. I recognized a local TV news reporter. I smiled as I walked toward the courtroom. Before I could say hi, he jabbed a microphone in my face.

"Are you the lawyer who sued Santa Claus?" His question caught me off-guard. The voice in my head said, *Oh, shit.*

Before I could think of a cute response, his cameraman flipped on a blinding camera light. "We hear you're calling the tooth fairy to testify for the family," the reporter grinned.

I felt a nip of shame, but I stuck out my chin, sidestepped the cameraman, and walked into the courtroom. Another local newscaster and her cameraman blocked my path to the judge's chambers. I locked eyes with Rita, the bailiff, sitting at her small desk next to the judge's bench.

"Where's the judge?" I asked self-consciously.

"He's in chambers, but he'll be on the bench in five minutes," Rita said.

Like hell he will, screeched the voice in my head. I knew the judge; he had given me a lot of leeway in his courtroom as a prosecutor.

"Interesting case, Jerry," Rita said, a little too cheerfully. "You never got this much attention trying murder cases."

I walked behind the bench, through the judge's private entrance and past his secretary, and poked my head into his office. "Hey judge," I whispered, "I got a problem." I knew I shouldn't be talking to the judge without the defense attorney's permission—ex parte communications are grounds for sanctions, but desperation got the best of me.

Judge Branson agreed to remove the TV cameras from the courtroom. He had no choice. At the time, both parties had to agree to televised legal proceedings, and I wasn't agreeing. But he wouldn't grant my wish to hold the pretrial in chambers, away from gawking court-watchers.

After a mundane ten-minute discussion in open court on the status of discovery and setting a trial date, I couldn't pack my briefcase fast enough. To paraphrase the humorist Kin Hubbard, "Next to the circus, there ain't nothin' that packs up and tears out of a courtroom faster than a humiliated young lawyer."

I double-timed it to the elevators, hit the down button, and waited impatiently to escape the humiliation. Hearing the ding of the arriving elevator behind me, I whirled around and barged past the sliding doors. As the doors closed, a prosecutor I knew well stuck his arm between the doors. The doors lurched back. "Hey Jerry," he shouted, "I thought the tooth fairy only worked nights."

"You're a dick," I yelled back.

Now I knew why Shafer had asked me to cover the pretrial. I don't recall how long it took to live down the ignominy of *Todaro v. Santa Claus,* but a generous paycheck suppressed self-pity. I wasn't ready for the precipitous fall of respect from fellow lawyers and people on the street. I don't know how long it took me to build that impenetrable wall protecting my emotional well-being from snarky remarks about personal injury lawyers. Mostly, I learned to deflect the insinuation that I had joined the ranks of blood-sucking lawyers, and my wife never complained when her friends, wives of doctors, suddenly became aloof.

12 The Difficult Judge

Lesson 12: Know your judge: stand your ground, but know when to back off and move on.

For all of us, we remember our first experience of something new or unusual. For me it was the wrongful death case for the widow Mary Larson. Forty-five years ago I stood behind the lectern, poised to give the jury my opening statement. I remember this moment clearly. "Any time, counsel," grumbled the judge.

My stomach was doing somersaults, my eardrums were pulsating, pounding louder and louder as I shuffled my notes. Did I say "poised"? Well, "scared shitless" best captures the moment.

Judge Fletcher made no effort to conceal his contempt. Only a year ago, I wore the white hat in the courtroom, prosecuting thieves and villains from the underbelly of the city. That morning, I might as well have climbed out of a bucket of scum, covered with green slime. Judge Fletcher glared at me. Instead of working on legal matters in chambers and clearing his backlogged docket, he had to sit in the courtroom for days listening to me, a contingency fee lawyer, trying to convince a jury to give his client's dead husband the key to the insurance company's strongbox. Judge Fletcher despised these cases and the lawyers who schlepped them into his courtroom. He saw me now as a blood-sucking plaintiff's lawyer.

A hostile judge spiked my blood pressure, but on the other side of the courtroom that morning, unchained, growling Dobermans masquerading as defense lawyers from a prestigious Columbus law firm sat ready, at the sound of the judge's gavel, to rip my face off.

Mary Larson's case was my first major civil trial; major because a jury could award over a million dollars. My client loved me. Why wouldn't she? She could get hundreds of thousands of dollars without paying a dime upfront to her lawyer. Despite my youth of 32 years (that's young for a trial lawyer), I dressed the part of a big firm lawyer—not like a flashy plaintiff's lawyer, sporting a beige sport coat and a Rolex dangling at the cuff of a powder blue shirt. Nope, I wore a charcoal gray pinstriped Brooks Brothers suit, a burgundy-colored tie over a starched button-down white shirt, and polished black wingtips.

My newly acquired look of a lawyer from a "white-shoe law firm" fit well in Columbus, but not so along the Ohio River in southern Ohio. In a trial two months before, the local defense lawyer in Pomeroy, Ohio, called me "the shiny-shoe lawyer from Columbus." But this morning I stood at center court, my back to Judge Fletcher, facing the jury in my carefully tailored professional image. That is, except for one hidden anatomical variant: My stomach had shrunk to the size of an egg.

Mary Larson's husband Lloyd made his living driving a flatbed truck mounted with a hydraulic boom to load and unload heavy equipment and construction materials. On the morning he died, he ate breakfast, kissed his wife, grabbed his lunch bucket, and drove his beater of a car to work. One of the jobs assigned to him that day was removing unused cement block at a construction site. Lloyd's truck was equipped with a handheld toggle that allowed him to stand outside the cab while raising and lowering the hydraulic boom.

He drove to the construction site, found the unused cement block, and secured the block on wooden pallets. He connected the first pallet to the boom's steel cable. As he maneuvered the pallet, the tip of the boom touched the lower of two overhead wires strung from a utility pole. *No problem*, Lloyd must have thought, as there were no sparks or flashes.

The pallet hung just below the floor of the flatbed, not high enough to transfer onto the truck bed. He pressed the toggle switch to lift the pallet higher. The boom grazed a second wire. Before he could blink, thousands of volts fried his brainstem. According to one of the construction workers who witnessed the incident, Lloyd landed on a pile of dirt, flames flickering from his shirt, "a smoldering heap of flesh."

The night before the Larson trial, I practiced my opening statement in front of the bathroom mirror, something I never had to do as a prosecutor. I changed the pitch and tone of my voice to trumpet the most compelling facts favoring my client, and deemphasize the negatives in a lower octave. By two in the morning, I could summarize the defendant's wrongdoing in five short, staccato sentences. I reworked my opening statement and reworded my cross-examination to minimize open-ended questions, such as any question beginning with the word "why"—a red flag of an inexperienced trial lawyer. I dreamed of a million-dollar verdict at the end of my maiden voyage.

Well-paid expert witnesses are the predominant force in civil cases for big money, and many of them testify frequently. Hired guns don't hesitate to take advantage of a poorly worded question. It's an opportunity to give a long-winded answer to attack the opponent's theories of liability. A series of questions calling for a simple yes or no on cross-examination is the mark of a skilled trial lawyer. I'd learned in my first civil trial that I could no longer count on the moral force of righteousness following me into the courtroom as a prosecutor, parting the seas of reasonable doubt. Persuading a jury—and my client's future—depended solely on the words that came out of my mouth.

I tried not to appear nervous. In his chambers, Judge Fletcher didn't hide his impatience with me. In the courtroom, the defense lawyers had their ears pinned back, and the jurors seemed to look right through me. As a prosecutor, jurors had smiled at me. I knew they saw me as their representative, and I could feel their respect and admiration. This morning, everywhere I looked I sensed disapproval and skepticism. Fear sucked the oxygen out of my chest. I was suffocating.

My plan was to win the case in my opening statement. I had learned from veteran civil trial lawyers to not only recite facts, but to plant the arguments that frame a picture of negligence in the juror's mind. Once the framework was crafted, the jurors would fit the evidence they heard into the story of liability mapped out in their heads. The mental storyboard would lead the jury down the path to award money to my client. Jury consultants tell us that jurors don't wait to hear all the evidence before making up their minds. Instead, after opening statements, jurors lean to one side or the other. By the time the golden-throated orator strolls to the lectern at the end of the evidence, adjusts his tie, clears his throat, and takes a sip of water, ready to deliver his *final* argument, individual jurors may have already decided who wins or loses.

As I mentioned, in the prosecutor's office I appreciated that justice meant different things to different people. But personal injury contestants battle over money, and injury lawyers measure justice in dollars and cents. Injury lawyers ask jurors to award a "full cup of justice," meaning all the money we ask for, never mind the one-third contingent fee. What jacked my heart rate that morning, more than I'd ever felt as a prosecutor, wasn't the fight for justice. It was the money. Justice is money. And there would be no justice for Mary unless I won.

In the prosecutor's office, I can only recall one night in three years that I lost sleep before a trial. I was trying my first murder case. Once I joined the ranks of plaintiff's lawyers, if I got more than three hours of sleep during trial, that was a good night. On the first morning of the Larson trial, 20 or so potential jurors had filled the seats in the back of the courtroom. As the bailiff called out the potential jurors' names, they solemnly took their assigned seats in the jury box, looking quizzically at the lawyers and their clients sitting at counsel table. I watched every juror walk to their seat. I had a good idea of how they spent the work week by the way they dressed. In the 70s, middle-aged women wearing dresses and blouses were predominantly housewives; men wearing work clothes or long-sleeved flannel shirts worked with their hands for a living. Any man wearing a sport coat and tie was marked for removal. No plaintiff's lawyer wants an unsympathetic businessman deciding how much money should be given to an uneducated working stiff.

I would try this case alone; no second-chair lawyer by my side passing me notes saying, "Ask this, ask that" or "Stop NOW." I still laugh when I recall what a senior prosecutor whispered to me during one of my first trials: "Shut the fuck up and sit down."

The young widow sat next to me at the counsel table. Her two small children were home with their grandmother. Mary Larson wore her church best, a plain, ankle-length red skirt. No jewelry. She was a bit on the heavy side, with a round face. The jury would like her. Mary held her hands in her lap, motionless, frozen in time and space. Sitting silently beside my client, I felt something strange, something I had never felt before, more than the usual pressure-cooker intensity of the courtroom. I could feel Mary's desperation. Unknowingly, I kept licking my lips; sandpaper lined the inside of my mouth.

Before being elected to judicial office, Judge Fletcher had made a living as an insurance defense lawyer. His conservative bent made him a prosecutor's dream. But for plaintiff's lawyers, Freddy Krueger in the movie *A Nightmare on Elm Street* comes to mind. Judge Fletcher was known to cut plaintiff's lawyers off at the knees and sweep their lawsuits from the courtroom with the slightest weakness in the evidence. It was a time when the slightest evidence of contributory negligence warranted dismissal. I knew even then that a judge could sabotage a lawyer's case by admitting or excluding hurtful or beneficial evidence, and my new bosses had warned me, "You are no longer the golden boy in the courtroom."

One of the first techniques I learned at a plaintiff's lawyer seminar on jury selection was *indoctrination*. The lawyer phrases a series of questions that creates a mental impression that anchors the jury to the plaintiff's theory in the case. I began jury selection with questions I had rehearsed the day before, designed to seed the silent and deadly dangers of electricity.

I asked a juror who seemed more talkative than the rest of the stone faces in the jury box, "Mr. Smith, have you had the experience of an unexpected electrical shock?"

I struggled to be more specific, adding examples of fiddling with a toaster or wiring in the basement. Before the juror could answer, Judge Fletcher leaned forward, both elbows on the top of the bench, head cradled between his hands. "Counsel," he barked, rancor dripping from his lips, "everyone knows you don't stick your hand in a rattlesnake cage."

I looked down at my legal pad as acid began bubbling in my stomach. The judge made me look like a young stupid lawyer, wasting the jury's time. I froze. I heard a snicker from one of the defense lawyers seated behind me. I didn't know what to do or what to say. Seconds passed in embarrassing silence, the judge's opinion marinating in the minds of the jurors. I couldn't immediately object and say, "You're being unfair, judge," or "It's improper to make statements to a jury that favors the defense side of the case." There's no such thing as a comeback when a judge castigates a lawyer in the courtroom. I had to stand there and take it. Judge Fletcher had planted a seed of his own. *Your client's a fool.*

During my three years in the prosecutor's office, no judge had abused me in the courtroom, attacking my intelligence or the validity of my arguments; not even Judge Fletcher, though he called my boss once, the chief prosecutor, and told him, "Todaro is gumming up the works." An ultra-aggressive prosecutor, trying case after case, week after week, alienated Judge Fletcher. When I was a young pup, a judge might tell me to "cut to the chase" or "you're finished with questions, right?" but always at the sidebar, outside the hearing of the jury.

The jury, of course, assumes the judge is the smartest lawyer in the room. If the judge criticizes the lawyer, the jury thinks the lawyer did something wrong. In Judge Fletcher's eyes, I stood for something different now. Not the lawyer for the state of Ohio fighting for justice, for the helpless and innocent victims of crime; I had joined those bottom-feeders looking for "pie in the sky"—a comment he made to me that morning as I walked from his chambers to the courtroom. Judge Fletcher's assault on my intellect and my credibility in the presence of the jury confirmed my underdog status in the courtroom.

A hostile judge and a desperate client were worry enough. Adding to the intimidating atmosphere were three defendants with two Dobermans each, a highly skilled defense lawyer and a second-chair lawyer to assist.

One of the defense lawyers who eyed my every move, anticipating where my questions were heading before I got there, was Charlie Brown. Four years earlier, he had successfully defended Ohio Governor Jim Rhodes in a federal lawsuit filed by the families of the students shot dead by Ohio National Guardsmen during an anti-Vietnam War protest at Kent State. Charlie, tall and broad-shouldered with jet-black hair and a prominent black mustache, had a commanding presence in the courtroom. His voice was powerful, authoritative, and indignant when deemed necessary. Standing next to him, I felt four feet high.

After a stressful jury selection, it was time for opening statements—my opportunity to present *my version of the truth*. I stood in the center of Judge Fletcher's courtroom, where I had stood countless times before, feet firmly planted, but I had the feeling I was standing on a trapdoor that would open the moment I provoked the judge. I struggled to find the starting point of my well-rehearsed opening statement. This time, Judge Fletcher called me by name: "Anytime now, Mr. Todaro." I focused on a housewife in the back row of the jury and began.

"Two years ago, the defendant, Columbus Construction, was the general contractor for a residential construction site. The general contractor is responsible for the safety of the working conditions at the building site. On the day Lloyd Larson died, he had to work below unprotected high-voltage wires. This was the dangerous condition lying in wait for Mr. Larson."

Charlie jumped to his feet, growling, "Ahhhbbb-jectionnnn, Your Honor, plaintiff's counsel is arguing his case—totally improper under the rules, Your Honor."

True, opening statements should not be argumentative. Lawyers must stick to telling the jury what facts they intend to prove, not conclusions on why they should win. The trick I learned was selecting and arranging information in a sequence that allows the facts to argue themselves. But Charlie didn't give a damn about the rules of opening statement. He didn't like its potential persuasive impact on the jury. So, he objected, but his true motive was disrupting the flow of my opening statement and unhinging my scripted, linear thought process. As I've mentioned, civil and criminal trials in America play out on a giant chessboard in the courtroom—documents and testimony are the chess pieces moved with the intent to capture a verdict. One gambit is intimidation, employed to knock your opponent off his game.

Jury consultants say that the first three minutes of opening statement is the critical time to grab the mind of the jury, and the initial 60 seconds of my opening focused the jury's attention on the danger created by the construction company. Given the judge's obvious favoritism, Charlie rightly assumed that the court would admonish me (again!) in front of the jury.

It worked.

Unethical? No. Gamesmanship? Yup. The judge, of course, agreed with Charlie.

"Opening statements are not the time for argument, Mr. Todaro," Judge Fletcher said contemptuously in front of the jury.

Savvy trial lawyers like Charlie Brown live on the edge of courtroom decorum; gamesmanship rules.

I walked nonchalantly back to the lectern, acting like nothing bad had happened; the jury would be watching my reaction. Charlie made me angry, and I was too rattled to think straight. I wasn't sure where I'd left off. Should I start over? I couldn't find a logical starting point. I stared at my outline for what seemed like minutes, my lungs inhaling the silence. Finally, I skipped over my carefully rehearsed scene of horrific death and began to speak. Instead of my face smiling back at me from my bathroom mirror, eight blank-faced jurors stared at me. I couldn't shake the telltale quiver in my voice. The rest of my opening statement lacked the passion and punch of hidden danger and a penniless widow. Instead, the jury heard a monotonous summary of facts and events.

On the second day of trial, I summoned to the witness stand an employee of the construction company. He was the first to run to Lloyd as he lay on the ground, clothes in flames. The witness couldn't say one way or the other whether he knew the tension wires were live, but he did say he didn't notice any protective rubber covering around the wires before Lloyd's death.

When Charlie rose to cross-examine the witness, he stood in the center of the courtroom. He faced the witness, hands clasped behind his back, feet shoulder-width apart, no legal pad and no notes. Charlie smiled. He didn't attack the witness like I would have; rather, he was friendly, as if he'd bumped into an acquaintance at the grocery store. He was courteous and his questions were conversational. After putting the witness at ease, Charlie asked if Lloyd was looking up at the boom when it touched the first wire. The witness replied that Lloyd stopped when the boom hit the first wire, but then he raised the boom again.

Charlie went for the jugular. "So you saw Mr. Larson continue to raise the boom while he was *looking* at the electrical wires?"

"Yes, sir."

"And those wires had no protective covering on them, isn't that right?"

"No."

"You mean, 'no, you didn't see anything covering the electrical wires'?"

"Yes, sir. That's correct."

Charlie looked directly at the jury, shrugged, and sat down.

At the end of the second day of the trial, I rested my case. Charlie immediately asked the judge to dismiss the plaintiff's case. The judge gave each side 30 minutes to argue the merits of the motion for dismissal outside the presence of the jury.

I argued that obviously Lloyd assumed the construction company had turned off the power and the wires weren't live. Charlie countered that Mr. Larson was responsible for his own death.

"Judge, he looked right at electrical wires. He saw they weren't covered or protected." Charlie pointed at the courtroom ceiling, then he borrowed the judge's scornful remark: "He might as well have stuck his hand in a rattlesnake cage."

The judge agreed.

Case dismissed.

Standing outside our office, Mrs. Larson dabbed the tears below her eyelids while she thanked me for all I had done. I had never felt this bad after losing a trial in the prosecutor's office. Her sad, helpless expression sent me spiraling down an emotional dark hole. It wasn't so much losing; I hated losing, but I had failed my client, and I hated myself. She was counting on me to change her life, and I had let her down. I knew how desperately she needed money to live, to keep her house.

I told Mary not to worry about litigation expenses; I knew she didn't have money to spare. I watched her walk to her car. She opened the car door, sat in the driver's seat, and leaned forward, resting her head on the steering wheel. I waited to wave goodbye. She didn't start the engine. I couldn't watch any longer. I went inside to face the partners.

"The judge fucked me," I told the senior partner. "I never had a chance. He threw me out before I got to the jury. Judge Fletcher is an asshole," I shouted, "and he berated me in front of the jury twice."

The senior partner sympathized with me as I paced back and forth in front of his desk, pointing out all of the times Judge Fletcher bushwhacked me. I wondered out loud whether I should have searched for more evidence on the lack of safety precautions at the work site. I sat down in the Chippendale chair in the corner of his office and complained about the one witness who had sunk my case. The eyewitness at the construction site might as well have held up a sign that said, "Lloyd was a dumbass."

The Larson case would not be the last time I would see a little bit of truth on both sides of a story. And it wouldn't be the last time that the lawyer with the better version of the truth got justice for their client. I had a lot to learn about trying complex civil cases, including that many times, hard facts and solid evidence are easily distorted by a juror's core values and unrecognized bias. In this case, personal responsibility was a core belief inside and outside the courtroom—at least it was back in the 70s.

Never, and I mean never, did I say a kind word about Judge Fletcher during his lifetime. To me, he represented an overbiased, defense-minded judge. If I had an injury case assigned to Judge Fletcher, I felt forced to settle. When I was a prosecutor, he tolerated me. Choosing to try another personal injury case in front of him would be suicide by stupidity.

Judge Fletcher died in 2007. Halfway into his obituary, I regretted every nasty remark I ever made about him. On D-Day, he'd parachuted into Sainte-Mère-Église, one of the first towns liberated by the American troops. I envisioned a college kid floating helplessly in the darkness, exposed to enemy gunfire, fighting back the fear of a bullet in the chest. He summoned courage, the depth of which I could only imagine. He'd fought in Operation Market Garden and the Battle of the Bulge. Frostbitten in his foxhole, he must have seen too many brave men die in harm's way, through no fault of their own. Too many men who couldn't be saved. Men long forgotten, but not by Judge Fletcher. I had never experienced the intense fear that my life was about to end, day after day. Judge Fletcher deserved my respect as a man.

Maybe the war had understandably hardened the judge against any man he believed had made a foolish assumption and wanted someone to pay for their mistake. Many years would pass before I better understood the many ways peoples' life experiences affect their judgment.

13 Telling the Truth Attractively

Lesson 13: Whether in a courtroom or a debate, it is critical to know the facts your opponent relies upon and the facts they ignore.

In the mid-1970s, a nuclear physicist at a local hospital failed to properly calculate radiation output on a colbalt-60 machine, and no one caught the error for months. One of Dan's clients, a young man diagnosed with non-Hodgkin's lymphoma, died four years after receiving radiation treatment. The hospital admitted negligence on the part of the physicist. Still, we had to prove that radiation killed our client, not cancer. I took the lead on putting the case together.

Except in rare circumstances, the standard of care and causation questions in medical malpractices cases must be answered by physicians in the form of an *opinion*. Individuals with specialized training or experience are permitted by the rules of evidence to assist the jury to draw conclusions about negligence, causation, and damages—the elements of an injury lawsuit. All of us see, hear, and read about the opinions of medical experts, probably every day. In many situations, there is little question about the expert's qualifications, although some experts are more qualified than others. But how experts arrive at their opinions . . . well, that's where the game begins.

Some experts see the glass as half full. Others have the maddening habit of seeing no glass at all, and finding fault in any bad outcome for a patient. Many defense experts will automatically defend a doctor's care, except in the most egregious cases. The true sense of impartiality in the average person is just as rare as it is in an expert witness. Many of today's litigation experts are experienced advocates, skilled at delivering varnished opinions in the courtroom for a fee.

Dan hunted for a pathologist who could provide an opinion that the patient had a shortened life expectancy and died a painful death from the overdose of radiation. The autopsy report stated our client died from lymphedema (lymphatic system blockage) and sepsis, but there was no mention of radiation damage to the lymphatic system. We hired a pathologist listed with one of the companies that provided expert witnesses for litigation. In the late 1970s, a cottage industry of medical search companies emerged, charging a fee for finding doctors willing to testify in medical malpractice cases.

At the meeting with our pathology expert, we pointed to the radiation overdose calculations. We wanted him to differentiate between the worsening malignancy of lymphoma and death caused by radiation. "We need to prove that radiation killed our client, not his cancer," Dan said. The pathologist knew what we were after; no reminder was necessary. He asked us to get tissue slides from the autopsy, as well as the official autopsy report.

It took over a month to get the tissue slides. Coroner's offices are cooperative, but sometimes the lack of manpower slows the process. We met again with our expensive pathologist in his Cleveland office to review his findings and hopefully to hear a favorable opinion on a radiation-induced death.

Our expert said this was an easy call. The autopsy showed severe scarring and damage to the lymph system and evidence of overwhelming infection. He was willing to write an opinion letter concluding, "Radiation damage destroyed the plaintiff's lymphatic system, leading to a lethal infection—the *immediate* cause of death."

"That's great," Dan said, "send us an invoice for your time along with your report."

After we shook hands and headed out of his office, the expert grabbed Dan by the arm. "Look," he said, "you should know that his lymphoma had a virulent cell type. If I'm asked, I will have to say that it carries a poor prognosis." We were not surprised by this revelation; we had already researched our client's cancer and knew the cell type of his lymphoma predicted a limited life expectancy. Dan asked if he could save that opinion for the courtroom. He agreed.

Before divulging evidence of the poor prognosis, the case was settled.

This radiation case was an initiation into the subtle forms of deception that play out in the courtroom. Expert witnesses may hide the ball if ethically possible, but they usually don't lie. Half-truths may have more influence than the whole truth. But if you are in this business long enough, you will see experts invent a theory that defies the prevailing view of sound medicine. The pathologist we hired provided an opinion that depended on the medical facts we asked him to assume. Lawyers in high-stakes malpractice litigation like to cherry-pick the medical facts that support their theory of the cause of injury or death. I didn't think anything was wrong with harvesting medical opinions with cherry-picked facts, until, of course, I started defending doctors. My doctor clients would call these experts liars; however, we humans have always hand-picked the information we want to believe.

I have rarely had a case where all the facts favor my client. A few medical experts will agree to ignore compelling facts and assume only those facts the lawyers suggest. When experts disregard too many pivotal facts relevant to assumptions and opinions, intellectual honesty suffers. Yet we lawyers call this "advocacy." My former partner, Frank Ray, a highly sought-after trial attorney who taught trial practice at Ohio State University Law School for a decade, jokingly calls this practice "telling the truth attractively."

14 Striking Out . . . On My Own

Lesson 14: If you're interested in maximizing your income and making a name for yourself in trial work, take the risk of building your own practice.

In my opinion, my medical knowledge and assistance in putting together the radiation case for Dan substantially contributed to a good settlement. It was time for Shafer & Higgins to make me a partner. Like anyone else who works hard for an employer and is responsible for the employer's business making a good profit, I saw myself as an indispensable lawyer in the investigation and preparation of medical malpractice cases.

Shafer & Higgins saw me as a worker bee.

For three years I often worked seven days a week, apart from the weekends of Ohio State home football games, holidays in Lakewood, New York, and long weekend ski trips to Killington, Vermont. What I didn't understand was the low replacement value of worker bees.

Rainmakers—lawyers who sign well-heeled clients and generate large fees—become partners. Associates grind out the hourly work. Part of an associates' fees go to the rainmaker who brings in the client, supervises the work, and sends out the invoice. The more associates the rainmaker keeps busy, the more generous (and some might say bloated) their annual salary becomes, and don't forget the annual bonuses. Associates grind away, make a reasonable salary, but don't share in the profits.

I left Shafer & Higgins three months later, thinking they were selfish and unappreciative. The lawyer who defended the hospital in the radiation lymphoma case worked for a prestigious trial law firm in Columbus. I thought his firm would be lucky to get a lawyer with my trial experience and medical training. When we met at a restaurant on the north side of town, he diplomatically explained that the new lexicon of law firms began with "eat what you kill," and the Columbus legal community was no exception. Lateral hires, experienced lawyers already in practice looking to change firms, had to bring a book of business to the table. Otherwise, the newly hired lawyer was just another mouth to feed. I was a wannabe lateral hire, with no clients and no book of business—a bad business hire.

Still, I was ready to leave Shafer & Higgins, but opening a law practice from scratch terrified me. Three years ago, I tried to join a startup law practice, and I bailed after two months. I agonized about cutting the umbilical cord of a biweekly salary. This move involved a leap of faith. I had leaped once already and fell on my face. How would I get cases? What would I do if no one sent injury cases my way? How would I pay my bills?

I'd seen what happened to lawyers who couldn't pay the rent. They worked from their homes. They used the courthouse law library for an office. I'd be one of those lawyers hanging around the courthouse at the weekly criminal arraignments, desperate for an appointment to represent indigent defendants. The hourly fees were ridiculously low. Known around the courthouse as "shoestring lawyers," they lived off the scraps of the legal system. Defending the destitute for a pittance didn't appeal to me.

Don Schumaker, a classmate at Capital and a respected criminal lawyer, lived primarily off courthouse appointments representing indigent defendants. Even today, court appointed lawyers in Columbus rake in a whopping $90 (up from $60) an hour (as of 2021) to defend indigent clients. Don fought for the rights of some of the most deranged minds served up by society. At the time of his death, Don was president of the Ohio Association of Criminal Defense Lawyers. The Association's announcement of his death noted he "represented forty-nine clients accused of capital murder," all by court appointment. Only one of his clients spent time on death row. What wasn't mentioned: Don's friends took up a collection to give him a decent funeral.

15 The Guilt of Overconfidence

Lesson 15: If after discovery is complete it is clear that your client doesn't deserve to win, settle out of court, if you can.

I joined two former prosecutors, sharing office space together. My office was no larger than a walk-in closet. I started contacting lawyers, setting up luncheon meetings, pitching for business, talking up my medical background. Slowly, lawyers began referring me injury cases. It wasn't my trial experience or reputation that motivated my referring lawyers. Nope; instead of sending referring lawyers the normal one-third contingency fee, I offered 50 percent. Sending 50 percent of my 40 percent contingent fee was a desperate move, but there was no other way to develop a plaintiff's law practice. At the time, lawyer advertising had just started, and was considered unseemly by members of the bar.

Mrs. Carlson, a middle-aged widow, lived with her 17-year-old son who had Down syndrome. Her husband died from an infected gallbladder and she never remarried. Hers was the first case I would try to a jury as a sole practitioner. Instead of Shafer & Higgins fronting the cost of litigation, I had to dip into my meager savings to pay for experts and deposition costs. For a sole practitioner, the business of paying my personal bills and covering the cost of litigation would provoke constant anxiety for the next 20 years—more stress than standing in front of a jury. I once heard an elderly plaintiff's lawyer say that the plaintiff's practice was like "walking on a highwire without a net."

Mrs. Carlson had lost three teeth due to chronic periodontal disease. Her hand-to-mouth existence didn't allow for major dental work. Even though her office visits were sporadic, my expert witness, Dr. James Burk, pointed out that the defendant had taken only sporadic X-rays, and his charting of the condition of her gums was both sketchy and infrequent.

"Evidence of negligence leaped off the pages of dental records," my expert said.

What's omitted from a patient's medical chart is one of the time-tested theories of negligence in malpractice lawsuits. Day one of a nurse's education begins with, "If it's not documented, it didn't happen." The doctor who claims on the witness stand that all vital signs were normal the morning before the patient died will be accused of fabrication, if a normal heart rate, blood pressure, and respiration rate are not contemporaneously documented on the patient's medical record. (Years later, on the defense side, I began to appreciate that doctors treat patients, not medical records. Overflowing emergency rooms and busy doctors' offices, coupled with patient demands, compromises completeness when it comes to recordkeeping.) When plaintiff's lawyers get a sniff of deficient charting, bloodhounds give chase on the litigation trail.

The week before Mrs. Carlson's trial, the defense counsel offered $7,500 to settle—a lowball offer. Sounding absolutely assured, I told Mrs. Carlson, "A jury will give you more money." I, Jerry Todaro, knew a winner when I saw one.

Mrs. Carlson readily agreed. She obviously thought that her lawyer must know what he was doing.

In the opening statement, I appealed to the jurors' sympathetic side. I explained that Mrs. Carlson's husband had died ten years after they were married; her son functioned at a fourth-grade level; she shuttled between work and constant care and advocating for her son. She couldn't always make it to the dentist.

The jury heard Dr. Burk explain that Mrs. Carlson's dentists failed to follow the basics of routine dental care. Thorough examination of the gums and dental X-rays catch the early signs of periodontitis—receding gum lines and infection beneath the gums. Early treatment avoids the loss of bones and teeth. Our evidence had gone well in front of the jury. Mrs. Carlson came across as a responsible mother making the best of a difficult life.

The defense lawyer's cross-examination zeroed in on a few gaps in her dental appointments.

Before final arguments, the defense lawyer bumped up the offer to settle at $10,000, a sign that he thought the jury was favoring Mrs. Carlson. Unless a patient dies in the dentist's chair, damages awarded in dental malpractice trials won't break the bank. But I was confident. "I think the jury will give us more," I told my client.

In final argument, using my best baritone, I described the footpath of dental malfeasance: gaps in X-ray studies, gaps in documentation, gaps in continuity of care. Gum disease and the loss of a few teeth is not the stuff of human tragedy, but I portrayed the life of a persevering woman, a mother caring for a disabled child, alone in the world, drawing down on her paltry savings only when medical care was necessary to save her health. Surely the jury would return a verdict of at least $100,000.

The defense lawyer argued that the plaintiff was predisposed to periodontal disease; it came on too quickly, closing the window for preventive treatment. He had blown up Mrs. Carlson's office chart on a large poster board, showing the jury her missed appointments and missed opportunities for treatment.

As the jury returned to their seats in the courtroom, none of the jurors looked in our direction. When I was a prosecutor, I didn't have to wait for the bailiff to read the verdict. If the jury found the defendant guilty, they wouldn't look at the defendant. If the jury avoided eye contact with my client, I knew I had lost.

It takes about five minutes for the judge to read over the jury's paperwork before announcing a verdict. This five-minute wait is the most anxiety-driven part of any trial. The courtroom is silent. My heart pounds. I used to genuinely fear I would have a heart attack, but 100 civil trials later, it's not quite the heart-stopping moment.

"Verdict for the defendant," the judge announced.

"Did we win?" Mrs. Carlson asked me.

Stunned, at first, I couldn't answer.

"No," I finally said. "We didn't."

I shook hands with defense counsel. He was my age. He congratulated me on trying a good case. He had played for Ohio State's basketball team—he knew how to win graciously.

Once a jury has rendered their verdict, jurors are free to discuss the case with the lawyers. Before they left the courtroom, I asked one of the female jurors why they found for the dentist. She replied that they felt my client was at fault because she didn't see her dentist regularly, and if she had, the dentist would have done a better job.

In the privacy of the small anteroom outside the courtroom, I explained to Mrs. Carlson what had happened. She broke down, sobbing. "Can we get the $10,000 back? I could use the money to paint my house."

The offer of settlement vanished after the defendant won. The money was gone. Unless the judge committed errors in handling the evidence, and he hadn't, there was no use appealing the jury's decision.

I drove Mrs. Carlson home. She lived in a blue-collar neighborhood in a home she and her husband had bought in the 50s. Homeowners parked their cars on the street. I parked in front of her house and as I gazed at her home, a spasm of guilt sickened me. One corner of the porch drooped, and the roof shingles curled at the edge. There wasn't a visible fleck of paint on her weathered, wood-framed house. If I had taken the $10,000, she would have had $5,000 after my fee and expenses. Money enough in 1981 to paint her house and fix her porch.

Mrs. Carlson stood by the driver's side of my car and told me she would stop by my office next week. She could pay the money she owed in installments. "Would that be OK?"

I told her she didn't owe me a penny, said goodbye, and drove off faster than the speed limit allowed. I couldn't drive fast enough.

I packed a few things and sulked my way four-and-a-half hours up I-71 to I-90 toward my hometown of Lakewood, New York. I stopped at Mike and Sam's, a popular college hangout during summer and semester breaks in nearby Jamestown. It was fall. Except for a few locals and a small TV in the corner of the bar, the place was quiet. I sat on a bar stool, ordered a draft, dropped 35 cents on the bar, and stared at the mirror behind the setup of cheap bar whiskey.

My gut kept sending the same the message: *You are a screw-up* (not exactly how I put it to myself). Mrs. Carlson had depended on me to make the right decision for her. Accepting the lowball offer of $10,000 would have been in her best interest. I had truly believed the jury would decide in my favor, and $10,000 was chump change to me. I hadn't taken the time to find out what was important to my client. Instead, I had been blinded by my fascination with bringing in a bigger verdict. I have to say that while I've repeated some mistakes more than once, going for top dollar over a client's best interests is not one of them.

I left Mike and Sam's. Drinking alone was not therapeutic. I stopped to see Ed Fagan, one of my best friends, a lawyer living in Jamestown. According to my mother, we'd known each other since the age of two. Ed had left a Wall Street law firm and took a thankless job in the Chautauqua County public defender's office.

One of the comforts of close friends is the freedom to confess your screw-ups without judgment. I brought beer. Ed drank coffee. He had sworn off drinking forever after waking up too many mornings not knowing what had happened the night before. Ed knew a thing or two about disappointment.

"Losing a trial is not a judgment on a lawyer's competency," he said, trying to console me and giving me a sober *been there, done that* smile. "I've lost trials for all kinds of reasons. The judge bulldozed my case, my client studied his shoelaces on the witness stand, or the prosecuting witness was up for canonization. I've had eyewitnesses so eager to get off the witness stand, they agreed with the prosecutor before he finished his question."

"Trial work," I replied, "is a grueling, tough business; long hours, a jealous mistress." I quoted Judge Fletcher's wisdom, imparted as we walked out of his chambers before the Mary Larson trial. "Boys," the judge said, "this is a helluva way to make a living."

"It's not the law that's hard," Ed laughed, "it's the people. When it comes to asking for money, juries look for all kinds of reasons not to forgive your client."

I understood. I had overlooked the effect of noncompliance on the jury. It wasn't that I failed to prove the dentist negligent, but in the eyes of the jury, my client didn't *deserve* to win.

When I finished the beer, I got up to leave. I told Ed it wasn't the defense verdict that hounded me, it was guilt. I would go back to my upscale condominium, in an upscale suburb, wash my Porsche on weekends, and move on to the next case. Mrs. Carlson would go back to her weather-beaten house, leaky roof, and front porch bowing to the street.

I wasn't married when I took Mrs. Carlson's case to trial. After I married a dreamboat (more on my wife Barb later), I began ever so slowly to learn that I was affected by "confirmation bias." I was so ensconced in my clients' corner that I suppressed the negatives of their personality and their faulty behavior, or saw reasonable decisions where most would say "that was stupid." I spent more time on my clients' positives. Intuitively, my dreamboat warned me about bad facts that I couldn't smooth over. I began to appreciate the moral instincts of the average person and, specifically, the average juror. When I started defending doctors, a few weeks before trial, I'd give Barb the gist of the plaintiff's and defendant's theories in the case. Her decision on who should win depended on the comparative worthiness of the doctor and the patient. Barb focused on personal behavior as well as the evidence. I have to say that she was rarely wrong. I'm not saying she is judgmental (no, I'm NOT), but being *deserving* has a lot to do with winning and losing in the courtroom.

I do worry about how my client will come across on the witness stand. Are they likeable? Did they lie about anything before taking the witness stand? Were they a compliant patient? And the absolute worse offense, did they exaggerate their injury or pain and suffering? The plaintiff runs the risk of offending a juror's sense of fairness and causing them to reject the case altogether.

In my years trying plaintiff's cases, I mistakenly believed that if the jury understood the medicine—the disease, its natural course, and the prevailing methods and treatment—that was enough to win. Not so—the behavior of the doctor and patient plays a much larger role in the decision of the jury. Arrogance is a deal-breaker in the courtroom. I tell my doctor clients, "It's not what you say, it's how you say it." When a doctor talks down to a jury, he (this is a male problem) should just toss his wallet to the jury foreperson and yell, "Take the money." Offending people who you want to do your bidding is a disaster in any setting, but in court, in the words of The Godfather, "It's the kiss of death."

Patients must come into the courtroom with "clean hands." This is probably no different than applying for a job. A heavy smoker, heavy drinker, and morbidly obese person has limited opportunities in the job market, despite federal laws prohibiting discrimination. Experienced trial lawyers don't count on antidiscrimination laws to protect their black American clients. Maybe personal issues are a result of a mental disorder, such as anxiety, depression, or post-traumatic stress, but even today, inside the courtroom and out, discriminatory attitudes prevail, and juries (consciously or unconsciously) ignore pleas of assistance from people they see as a lesser version of themselves. In my opinion, people tend to see themselves as better and smarter than their neighbor. We are very quick to point out the mistakes others make. Of course, criminal behavior is the exception to overemphasizing a person's personal deficiencies. The demonization of Jeffrey Epstein has lasted for years.

I needed to start spending as much time justifying my injured client's behavior as I did on the doctor's negligence. I learned that my clients had to meet the expectations of the average person on the street. I had to see my client the way a juror sees themselves. I would learn from jury consultants that jury duty brought out a quirk in human behavior. Despite the doctor telling the plaintiffs that their symptoms were nothing to worry about, jurors say to themselves, "*I* would have gone back to the doctor at the first sign of their return." When we see someone make a serious mistake, our reflexive protective mechanism reacts by saying, "I wouldn't let this happen to me. I wouldn't end up dead." I had to show the jurors they would have done the same thing. I had to show the average juror that my client was vulnerable, just like them.

Looking back, I would have spent more time having Mrs. Carlson talk about the lack of explanations from the defendant dentist about her ongoing dental problem, his failure to proactively address periodontal disease, and what she would have done if she had been provided with the warning signs of gum disease.

16 How to Act Like a Pro

Lesson 16: Jurors are unmoved by trial lawyers' personal attacks on each other.

On the morning of another trial—like most trials—there was a moment of stillness in the courtroom. Opposite forces sat a few feet apart, filling the air with a static electrical charge. The courtroom setting could have passed for a still photograph captioned "Calm before the storm," with billowing black clouds and lightning bolts hovering over the room, though lawyers like to refer to this setting as "two scorpions in a bottle."

The youth pastor, in his late 20s, sat next to me. He was dressed in a white shirt, tie, and blue blazer. The judge sat behind the bench, whispering instructions to his bailiff. The defendant doctor sat next to defense counsel, hypnotically transfixed on the plaque of the state seal of Ohio on the opposite wall of the courtroom. The defense attorney stared intently at a black binder of medical records—ignoring the court, the jury, and me.

The court reporter, seated close to the witness stand, busied herself feeding steno paper into her stenograph machine. Eight expressionless jurors and one alternate sat quietly in the jury box, shifting glances from the lawyers and the defendant doctor to my client and the judge. What were they thinking? Could they see my brain squirming?

My client turned to me and said, "You could cut the air in here with a knife."

Only after winning will a lawyer talk about the pleasure of taking a case to trial. Lawyers love to embellish the moment they paint a witness into a corner—small triumphs that morphed into the smoking gun that won the case. When we lose, there's no bluster, no entertaining stories to be told. Any lawyer who tells me how much they enjoyed trying a case while in trial—well frankly, he's *plein de merde*. There may be a brief sense of euphoria when the other side blunders or when I have a Perry Mason moment, but for me and the other lawyers who hate losing and care about their clients and face the prospect of a major financial loss, anxiety and fatigue are constant companions throughout every waking hour during trial.

In the middle of the trial, my youth pastor client asked, "How do you do this day after day?"

His wife, a young woman named Beth, died during the delivery of her first child when she developed pregnancy-induced hypertension (today, doctors call hypertensive disorders caused by pregnancy *gestational hypertension*). Weeks before Beth's due date, her prenatal records showed a gradual rise of blood pressure to a dangerous level and high levels of protein in her urine, a concern that her kidneys were not filtering properly.

Two days before her death, Beth saw Dr. Reynolds and complained of blurred vision and pain in her belly. According to my expert, a high-risk perinatologist, elevated blood pressure, protein in urine, abdominal pain, and blurred vision were classic symptoms of severe preeclampsia. If a mother-to-be with preeclampsia has a seizure, she has reached the stage of eclampsia, a lethal condition for both mother and baby.

The emergency squad records revealed Beth had had a seizure at home.

When Beth arrived at the hospital, the emergency room physician immediately gave her magnesium sulfate and made an urgent call to Dr. Reynolds. Reynolds rushed to the hospital and performed an emergency C-section, but it was too late. The mother died. The baby lived.

Gary Stafford defended Dr. Reynolds. I cringed when I read his name on the pleadings. He might as well have been the Prince of Darkness himself. Stafford was a gladiator in the courtroom; fearless, aggressive, and nasty, showing no respect for opposing counsel or judges. He didn't cross-examine medical experts; he attacked them. In final arguments, he called plaintiff's experts "paid mercenaries," "professional prostitutes," and "liars." He'd win. Appellate courts had reversed some of Stafford's favorable verdicts because of inflammatory final arguments. Undeterred,

Stafford would try the case again, toning down the "inflammatory" rhetoric and still managing to win.

Plaintiff's experts feared Stafford's command of medicine. Stafford consumed medical knowledge. He knew as much about the condition, diagnosis, treatment, and outcomes as the doctors he challenged, and experts sensed they were facing a lawyer they couldn't bullshit. Stafford studied medical literature and found alternative diagnoses that would exonerate his client. It was rumored that he told his doctor clients to shut up and stay out of his way. I feared Stafford.

Stafford had built his defense around the testimony of his medical expert, a "hired gun"—doctors who testify around the country for a princely fee. His expert had relied on what my expert considered an outdated theory of medical management to defend Dr. Reynolds. If lawyers could lay their hands on past transcripts of an expert witness's testimony, they might find opinions inconsistent with the expert's theory of negligence in the present case. I had obtained two transcripts that contained statements by this expert that contradicted his theories of negligence in our case.

When I cross-examined Stafford's expert, he couldn't remember his testimony in the previous cases. I read his contradictory opinions to him and the jury. This technique is used every night on CNN and Fox News. He sputtered, unable to explain or reconcile his different opinions on management of preeclampsia.

After we had finished the day, I waited at the elevator to descend to the first floor of the courthouse. The defense expert walked up to me.

"It's not fair to ask me about my testimony in cases from ten years ago," he said, obviously miffed. "No one can remember the facts of a case that far back. My opinions were appropriate for the facts in that case." He continued angrily, "You were taking my testimony out of context."

There was a bit of truth there, but I didn't care. To me, he was a hired gun. It was me against him. I had a client to represent and nothing he could say would convince me that he was not disingenuous.

Before the trial, I knew I had to elevate my game to match up with Stafford. I had read all the medical literature. I had to research his expert's past testimony. I had to get in the expert's face and accuse him of trickery. And I had to make sure I had the evidence to prove the expert's statements were contradictory. In final argument, I pointed at Stafford and accused him of orchestrating a bogus defense.

At the time I went to trial against Gary Stafford, rumor had it that he'd tried 30 cases and won all but one of them. I can't say the plaintiff's verdict made me famous. However, my self-esteem exploded when I entered the elite million-dollar club. Even plaintiff's trial lawyers from Cleveland (the big-city trial attorneys hovering over us lesser-lights from Columbus and Cincinnati) congratulated me. Moreso because, in their eyes, I'd bested Stafford.

I talked with the jurors after the trial. Some of the women on the jury told me that they expected the lawyers to be passionate, but they really didn't like the name calling and the accusations of misconduct Stafford and I hurled at each other.

Less than a year later, after Stafford deposed one of my experts in an anesthesia case, we shared the backseat of a taxi to the Boston airport. I felt awkward sitting next to the lawyer I had slammed in front of a jury just months ago.

"Since the Reynolds case, my stock as a trial lawyer has skyrocketed," I told him, thinking he might be flattered. I also felt it necessary to apologize for calling him everything but a liar in final argument.

"You don't owe me an apology," he said, looking out at the Boston skyline from the backseat window of the cab. I could tell he meant it. That was it—not another word the rest of the way to the airport. No banter, nothing of the usual friendly but semi-sincere comments like, "You did a great job cross-examining the witnesses." We split the cost of the cab fare and split from each other, lugging our oversized briefcases filled with medical books to the ticket counter.

At the airport restaurant, I ordered a glass of red wine, a bowl of New England clam chowder, and extra oyster crackers. While I watched the little crackers bob in the soup, I thought *this is how a pro handles defeat*, the same way Jim O'Grady seemed unfazed when he lost a high-profile murder case. I couldn't remember O'Grady castigating a jury or a defense lawyer when we gathered after a trial at our watering hole across the street from the courthouse. I don't remember Jim blaming the judge, though at times there were good reasons to deflect blame. Stafford expected a fight in the courtroom. He expected I would use every argument possible to win, and it was his job to do the same.

I had asked a lawyer in Stafford's firm what he had to say after the case. "Shit happens." That was it.

On the flight home that night, the juror's criticism kept rolling around in my mind. I decided I would try to be more professional, embrace defeat and learn from it, and not complain about the opposing lawyer. And, I decided that if I had to be critical of a lawyer in the courtroom, I would criticize their arguments and conclusions and avoid all personal attacks. I've tried to maintain this attitude outside the courtroom too, but sometimes my frustration with juries gets in the way of the best version of myself.

17 So You Want to Be a Plaintiff's Trial Lawyer?

Lesson 17: Trial lawyers not only battle each other; they grapple with stress and fatigue. It's best to exercise regularly to maintain stamina.

On our second anniversary, my dreamboat was pregnant with our second child. We had moved into an upscale suburb of Columbus. A hefty mortgage, one baby, another on the way, and my practice was taking on serious injury cases. I'd wake up at three in the morning and start thinking about a problem in one of my cases. Unable to get back to sleep, I would drive to my office.

Our second child was due in September. In mid-July, I woke up in the middle of the night. My chest hurt. My dad had had a heart attack at 55. Even though I was just 41, I was sure I was destined to have one. Any time I experienced chest pain, I mulled over a quick trip to an emergency room.

At daybreak, I called a doctor friend at Ohio State. He got me in the same day. Tests were ordered, looking for every possible malady responsible for chest pain. There was a blood test, a stress test, a barium study of my intestinal tract, even an endoscope down my throat looking for a stomach ulcer. I had a resting EKG, then I ran on a treadmill hooked up to an EKG. I've been a runner and cyclist since law school. I ran 15 minutes and 59 seconds, 1 second shy of stage 4 on the Bruce Protocol, even though the nurse monitoring my heart rate started yelling, "He's at 200, HE'S AT 200."

After the treadmill test, the cardiologist told me, "I don't know what's causing your chest pain, but a person with heart problems can't run the rubber off the treadmill."

An hour later, my doctor friend sat down with me in his office and asked what was going on in my life. "Nothing physically wrong with you," he said, shrugging his shoulders.

I told him my cases involved severe injuries: brain trauma, dead spouses, and the worst, dead children. My clients signed up with me because they thought I was the best lawyer to right a wrong. They expected retribution and expected me to get it.

I fretted about my cases after work, on weekends, and in the middle of the night. "Everything comes down to money," I said. "I have a line of credit with a bank to finance my cases and it's nearly maxed out. I worry about losing. If I lose at trial, my investment in the case is gone and my strapped clients can't pay me back." I explained how I worried about what would happen if I couldn't pay my bills. "One minute a case is going great, the next minute new evidence sends the prospect of settlement tumbling down an elevator shaft."

I whined about judges. Inexperienced lawyers who couldn't make it in private practice were getting judicial appointments. Their lack of skill was a headache for trial lawyers and it was a frustration that most lawyers endured because calling out judges could affect your next case in front of the that judge.

"Some judges are more concerned about clearing their docket than spending time in the courtroom trying cases. I worry about a judge summarily dismissing my case before I get in front of a jury." This was a constant bitter complaint I didn't mind sharing.

"A judge can do that?" he asked, giving me a quizzical look.

"Yes, they can. Two weeks before last Christmas, the defense lawyer in one of my big cases was ready to offer me $800,000, but the judge dismissed the case. She was known for clearing her docket before the end of the year."

I told my doctor I had a hard time keeping my mind on my personal life. "We'll be out for dinner and Barb will bristle, 'I'm talking to you, Jerry.' But my mind had drifted off to a telephone call from my expert who raised a problem that could derail my case." I wasn't sure I was a good husband. "Last week," I told him, "I'm in a movie theater with Barb and her high school friend visiting for the weekend. One minute I'm fascinated, watching flight deck operations on an aircraft carrier; the next minute, my heart tried to jump out of my chest. I wanted to run out of the theater. The ground seems to constantly shift under my feet. I can't find my footing."

"Panic attack," the doctor said. "You need a vacation."

"Can you write a prescription for a week in the Bahamas without wife and child?"

"Well, whatever you want," he said, laughing. "You may need the name of my divorce lawyer, too."

I didn't have any singular passion for social issues when I entered law school. As I look back, trial lawyers were the center of my attention, and I liked the glory of saving the day for the underdog. I had no idea of the stress involved. In years to come, I would suffer headaches, but the head CT scans were negative; I had eardrum spasms before a trial, but all tests were negative; I had sudden bouts of flu symptoms and stomach pain, only to have them disappear in 24 hours the week before trial. Finally, I stopped going to doctors except for flu symptoms and debilitating back pain. It was too embarrassing. When I was sure I had a terminal disease, my wife would ask if I was going to the Mayo Clinic or if she should make an appointment for me at Massachusetts General Hospital in Boston.

In late-night sessions, sharing beers with other plaintiff's lawyers, it helped to know that fear, anxiety, and bitter disappointment was a plaintiff's trial lawyer's constant companion. What was *not* a topic of conversation was our personal interest tethered to the outcome of every case. *We were masters of turning painful and permanent injuries into a payload of cash.* Lose at trial, and not only does the client walk away with nothing, which hurts, but I could lose a hundred thousand dollars of my own money. My injured clients and widows struggling to pay their mortgages and feed their children were in no position to pay back money advanced for litigation costs. For a sole practitioner, a plaintiff's medical malpractice lawyer, high-stakes gambling became a fretful way of life.

When I started law school, I dreamed of glory. The reality of the courtroom changed my aspirations of fame and recognition to fear of failure and an acidic intestinal tract, but my body floated in the courtroom when a jury announced a plaintiff's verdict.

My experience is not unique. Trial lawyers set themselves apart from every other licensed lawyer on the planet. They embrace adversity. They have courtroom skills, engaging personalities, aggressiveness, nerve, and an aptitude capable of overcoming the fear that sucks the will from most lawyers' souls. As for me, a sole practitioner sharing office expenses under gut-heaving stress, the thrills came with the occasional plaintiff's verdict and settlement checks. It was like, as Melvin Belli once said, "The angels sing, and cash registers ring."

I could go nose-to-nose against the best defense lawyers and Ivy League experts. I could even face the bane of all trial lawyers, inexperienced and mediocre lawyers ill-suited for judicial office. Through it all, exercising to exhaustion, the joy of our children, and a gifted, multitasking wife have allowed me to keep my sanity. Yet, just as importantly, I've had partners and soulmates that have picked me up when I've fallen.

Sometime in the late 1980s, when my practice was running well and I felt my reputation unassailable among the plaintiff's bar, I distinctly remember the evening when reality slapped me hard across the side of the head.

The blow came in a brief car ride with Jack Anderson, the investigative journalist and nationally famous newspaper columnist. The Columbus Bar Association's doctor-lawyer committee hosted its annual dinner for doctors and their wives, to dispel the rumor circulating in the medical community that lawyers shared office space with Satan himself. My responsibility was to pick up the evening speaker, Mr. Anderson, at the airport.

For all his fame as a muckraking journalist, Mr. Anderson seemed like a regular guy. Round-faced with receding white hair, his rumpled suit was overdue for a visit to the dry cleaners. He smiled graciously and thanked me for picking him up.

On the way to the hotel, he asked me, "What kind of car is this?" He sounded sincere.

"It's a Porsche," I said.

"Oh," he said, and then asked me who made the car.

I mentioned the Germans and changed the subject. *Are you kidding me? A nationally famous journalist from Washington, D.C. doesn't recognize a Porsche or know that it's German-made?*

I asked Mr. Anderson whether he had lawyers on his staff, and what they did.

He said they helped with fact investigations and kept him from getting sued. Mr. Anderson turned to me and asked what I did.

I decided it was better not to announce that I sued doctors and told him I did personal injury work.

In a grave voice, looking straight ahead as my Porsche effortlessly chewed up the pavement, he said, "Lawyers are gravel in the road."

Goddamn. Is there anyone out there except my wife, mother, and children who don't despise me?

As the years passed, something unexpected happened. I saw less and less of what I deemed medical malpractice. Bad results after surgery didn't mean the doctor was at fault. Turning away clients required skillful management of honest people genuinely assuming someone must be at fault. The worst was telling the guilt-ridden parents of a dead child that they didn't have a case against a doctor who hadn't suspected a fatal disease. Potential clients found it hard to believe—unacceptable actually—that blame ultimately fell on the body's inability to ward off a disease. They assumed the doctor must have made a mistake. "It's not OK to make a mistake—not on me, not on my child," was my clients' unspoken assumption. I always felt the spirit of Christmas when I handed a sizable check to my clients. But I never got used to being the skunk at the lawn party.

18 Witness Intimidation

Lesson 18: Preparation of one's client for trial includes anticipation of your opponent's intimidation tactics—for witnesses, be ready to find a backup.

Healthy babies "pink up" immediately after delivery. Little Sonya did, too. But something wasn't right. Sonya's mom could tell, even though this was her firstborn. Sonya's nostrils flared when she tried to breathe. A local cardiologist found a hole between the left and right ventricle of her heart, the heart's two major pumping chambers.

Sonya had been born with a large ventricular septal defect (VSD). The hole between the two pumping chambers allowed deoxygenated blood to freely mix with her oxygenated blood. The left chamber, the workhorse of the four chambers in the heart, pumped less oxygen-rich blood to the body, while at the same time forcing too much blood into the lungs, at pressures higher than her tiny arteries could manage. Sonya's miniature arteries went into constriction mode to reduce blood flow to the lungs. It's like puckering your throat if you tried to drink out of a garden hose gushing water. Less oxygenated blood to the rest of her body meant little Sonya tired easily.

Frequently, children born with a small VSD don't require surgery and the hole closes on its own. But with larger holes, over time, the constant constriction of the immature arteries in the lungs causes them to become fibrotic and harden. Uncorrected, a child has a limited life expectancy.

The large hole in Sonya's heart needed a patch—a delicate, technically demanding surgery.

Sonya came under the care of Dr. Burch, an aging pediatric cardiovascular surgeon. Dr. Burch waited six months to allow Sonya to grow, to better handle the stress of surgery. Instead of patching the hole in her heart, he surgically placed a tight band around the pulmonary artery, the vessel transporting the deoxygenated blood from the right ventricle to the lungs. The idea behind banding was to normalize blood flow to the lungs and protect the tiny arteries. By age three, Sonya struggled to gain weight and tired easily. Her mother limited her playtime.

During one of her hospital checkups, Sonya's mother asked a young doctor, "Isn't there something more that can be done?"

The young pediatric cardiologist, just out of training, quietly suggested she contact a surgeon at Boston Children's Hospital.

Sonya's mother asked, "Do we really have to go that far?"

"You should see a lawyer, too," the words slipped out of the corner of his mouth.

Sonya's parents packed medical records and their weakened three-year-old into their car and drove to Boston's Children's Hospital, recognized internationally as a center for treatment of children with rare medical conditions.

Tests in Boston showed early signs of damage to Sonya's lungs. Dr. Aldo Castaneda, a pediatric cardiovascular surgeon and pioneer in repairing congenital heart defects, met with Sonya's parents. He told them he could remove the band and try to patch the hole between the two ventricles. He felt confident he could improve Sonya's quality of life. He was less confident, he told them, that the procedure would reverse the damage already done. A month later, Sonya was home and breathing better. Her short-term prognosis much improved, but long-term was a question mark. The damaged vascular system in her lungs might falter as she reached adulthood, reducing her life expectancy.

Anger motivates patients who believe they have been wronged by a doctor. I've heard clients say, "This doctor should have his license taken away," or "I'm not in this for the money, I just don't want this to happen to someone else." My immediate response to the more noble reasons for suing the medical profession and the doctor they once trusted? "A malpractice lawsuit is only about money. If I sue the doctor, the medical board is not going to yank the doctor's license. Nor will the hospital take away the doctor's privileges. Will we change the doctor's method of practice? Highly unlikely." Despite lawyer advertisements on television and billboards marketing injured people's legal right to *justice*, malpractice and personal injury lawsuits are about money—only about money. My thought process involved a business calculation. Is the case worth my time and expense? Will I be able to put money in my client's pocket and in my bank account? That's all *I* can do.

The red flag I searched for in Sonya's medical records waved brightly in Dr. Castaneda's operative note, dictated after Sonya's surgery. Occasionally, surgeons summoned to operate on critically ill patients transferred from an outside hospital write a self-serving sentence in the patient's medical chart. More often, a healthcare provider tells the patient privately, "If only you would have come here sooner."

In Dr. Castaneda's notes in Sonya's medical records, he described anatomical abnormalities that were not mentioned in Dr. Burch's operative note. Dr. Castaneda recommended patching the VSD. The passage of time limited the benefit of a corrective procedure, but closing the hole in her heart would improve her normal daily activities.

To me, the message was clear. Instead of simply banding the pulmonary artery, the hole in the wall between the two chambers should have been closed. Sonya's medical records became the blueprint for a medical malpractice suit. I called Dr. Castaneda's office and asked for a face-to-face conference.

Dr. Castaneda's operative note was not a smoking gun, but more like picking up the scent of prey; a bloodhound unleashed.

Because of the high mortality rate of malpractice cases in the courtroom, my goal was always out-of-court settlements. Plaintiffs lost in trial 80 to 90 percent of the time. It's no secret that jurors give the doctor the benefit of a doubt (after COVID, the public's attitude toward doctors changed dramatically).

Jurors came up with all kinds of reasons to favor the doctor: "He did the best he could," or "The doctor was young; we didn't want to put a black mark on his record." The most frustrating was "The doctor didn't intentionally injure the plaintiff, so we couldn't find him guilty." Civil cases have nothing to do with guilt or innocence. After years of jurors finding against me, I had come to the belief that the old guard of trial lawyers was right: "If the facts don't pass the puke test, don't take the case."

Unless insurance companies fear losing, they refuse to settle out of court or may only offer chump change. When I started in the malpractice business, I thought filing what I believed were meritorious cases supported by highly credentialed experts would force insurance companies to their knees. That rarely worked. One successful method I used involved getting the subsequent-treating doctors to testify against the defendant doctor. Not surprisingly, only a small percentage of treating doctors cooperated with me, especially if the defendant physician referred patients to the treating doctor or their practice group. Doctors infrequently bite the hand that feeds them.

Jurors and the general public believe, for good reason, that doctors won't testify against each other. But if the subsequent-treating doctor, not a hired expert witness, raises his right hand on the witness stand and testifies, "I'm here because it's the right thing to do for my patient," the defense lawyer might be heard humming that Willie Nelson tune, "Turn out the lights, the party is over."

Outside the entrance of Dr. Castaneda's waiting room was a row of chairs. I sat there sipping coffee, thinking over the best way to cajole him into becoming an expert witness. Promptly at 9:00 a.m. I introduced myself to his secretary, and she ushered me into his spacious office. Dr. Castaneda, a slight man of Guatemalan heritage in his early 50s, greeted me like his favorite patient. I told him I'd read one of his book chapters on heart defects. I had. We talked about his work for a good five minutes, about the difficulty and challenge of treating infants with heart defects. He got up from behind his desk. *OK,* I thought, *my time is up.* Instead, he grabbed my elbow and led me to the back wall of his spacious office, lined with gray metal cabinets. He pulled out the files of children with heart defects, explaining the technical struggle to mend what only a decade ago was unfixable. I wanted to stop him and say, "I know who you are; you don't have to prove anything to me." I was flattered that he thought it was important that I understood his commitment to help so many unfortunate children.

Finally, I brought up little Sonya, and mentioned his repair of her heart. Dr. Castaneda seemed puzzled that Dr. Burch hadn't repaired the hole in the septum. He agreed that banding the pulmonary artery was not as effective as patching the defect. He agreed that the standard of care required closing the septal defect, and if Dr. Burch didn't have the capability to correct the defect, that the standard of care required transfer of Sonya to a facility with doctors able to perform the surgery needed.

I flew back to Columbus, ecstatic. Dr. Castaneda and I were tight. I had in hand a world-class expert the defense could not top. No doubt this case would settle. I immediately drafted a letter to Dr. Burch's defense counsel naming Dr. Castaneda, chief of pediatric cardiovascular surgery at Boston Children's Hospital, as my expert witness. I sprinkled in his position as a full professor at Harvard School of Medicine—an attention-getter, as my dad would say, after giving me a gentle whack behind my head for misbehavior (a daily occurrence until the age of 12).

As expected, I received a letter from defense counsel asking for the deposition of Dr. Castaneda.

Two months later, I walked down the corridor leading to Dr. Castaneda's office for our scheduled prep for his deposition. The moment I opened the door to Dr. Castaneda's waiting room, I saw Dr. Burch and defense counsel chatting with the secretary and sipping from Harvard-crested coffee cups. The Windsor knot around my neck suddenly tightened like a coiled boa constrictor. They had already introduced themselves to Dr. Castaneda, handshakes all around, I assumed.

"Dr. Castaneda is ready for you," his secretary said. Defense counsel said they would come back at the allotted time for the deposition. The secretary asked if I wanted coffee. I didn't. I felt sick to my stomach. She closed the door behind me. The once pleasant, gracious physician appeared stiff and uncomfortable. Dr. Burch was no longer just a name on a page from a Midwestern backwater town, unequipped to perform advanced surgical techniques. The name now had a face, a heart, and sucked air into his lungs—an agitated colleague sitting in the room ready to stare down Dr. Castaneda and later spite his reputation.

Dr. Castaneda, his face covered with regret, said he'd rather not testify. "Banding," he said, "is not what I would have done, but it's a reasonable procedure to do. Dr. Burch did the best he could."

The conversation lasted five minutes.

I canceled the deposition. I had no choice. Forcing an unwilling physician to testify in a malpractice case is sheer stupidity. At best, Dr. Castaneda would recount his treatment and its improvement of heart function but deny that he had any opinions one way or another about Dr. Burch's medical care. However, skillful defense lawyers know how to tap into a doctor's store of knowledge that leads down the yellow brick road. I knew the drill. If I went forward with the deposition, inevitably Dr. Burch's lawyer would get to this line of questioning:

Q. Aren't the lungs at risk for damage in infants with VSD?

A. Yes.

Q. Isn't protection of the lungs necessary treatment in VSD?

A. Yes.

Q. Isn't it true that medical texts and published medical literature document two or three options of treatment to relieve pressure in the lungs?

A. Yes, but I prefer patching the septal defect.

Q. Isn't banding the pulmonary artery one of the options of treatment approved in the medical literature?

A. Not the one I use, but banding is an option.

Q. According to medical literature, isn't banding the pulmonary artery a *reasonable option* of treatment for patients with VSD?

A. Yes.

Q. And you saw in Sonya's records Dr. Burch banded the pulmonary artery, didn't you?

A. Yes . . . he did.

Q. So isn't it fair to say that Dr. Burch acted reasonably when he opted to band the pulmonary artery?

A. Yes.

If I'd gone forward with Dr. Castaneda's deposition, I would have handed the defense attorney a powerful expert witness that I couldn't counter. Led by the defense attorney, Dr. Castaneda would have constructed a one-way street, guided by reflective road studs leading the jury to a defense verdict.

I dreaded meeting with Sonya's parents. After my first meeting with Dr. Castaneda, I had raised their hopes and fed their imagination with images of financial support for Sonya as she grew older. Now all their dreams would crash inside my office, and I was responsible. I had misled them; I had failed them. But Sonya's parents were not my typical clients. They decided to dismiss the case. Focusing on Sonya's health, they said, was more important than the lawsuit.

Intimidation tactics play out every day in litigation. If I didn't have a medical expert to prove that the defendant doctor breached the standard of care, the judge would be required to dismiss the case. Fear, at some level, seems to be the root element of intimidation. For Dr. Castaneda, criticism from his peers backed him away from the witness stand. It never occurred to me that a surgeon with a national reputation would fear criticism. Condemnation bounces off when it comes from individuals who are at odds with our line of work, but denunciation by our peers, and the loss of respect, has a powerful influence on our behavior. After Sonya's case, I tried to tactfully remind the treating doctors that I persuaded to testify in medical malpractice cases to confirm their willingness to serve as an expert witness with the knowledge that the defendant doctor might show up at the deposition—stare them down, act disgusted, shake their head in disagreement, or jab an index finger at hastily scribbled notes while the defense lawyer asks questions. I came to the realization that despite my woodshedding, even thick-skinned individuals shrink from peer criticism.

It's uncommon that treating doctors offer opinions on standard of care in a malpractice case. In the early 1980s, experts-for-hire solved this problem.

The difference between the best care and reasonable care was a distinction I failed to appreciate before Sonya's case. Years later, on the defense side, I would watch skilled plaintiff's lawyers tap into jurors' personal desire for the best care, and transform jurors' thinking to see reasonable medical care as having failed their patient—the common technique of putting jurors in the shoes of the plaintiff so that they see the world through their lens.

19 Hired Guns

Lesson 19: In short, medical experts who testify frequently see the big picture and seldom allow counsel to paint them into a corner. On cross examination, the use of medical literature and pointing out the facts they ignore may be the only tactic. Surprisingly, showing the jury the expert's high fees has no effect.

In the 1970s, it was easier to buy plutonium on the black market than finding a treating doctor to willingly—even if handsomely paid—accuse a colleague of malpractice. It was the so-called code of silence. Malpractice lawsuits require medical expert testimony. With rare exceptions, a lawsuit cannot proceed in court without a doctor offering an opinion that the defendant doctor fell below the standard of care. Unlike auto accident cases, where a bright yellow line on the highway marks the difference between right and wrong, medical malpractice requires a medical doctor in the same or similar specialty to establish medical care was left of center of the yellow line of fault.

By the early 1980s, private companies emerged, forming a spin-off cottage industry of medical experts-for-hire who were willing to testify in medical malpractice cases, almost entirely for plaintiff's lawyers. Defense lawyers had to knock on a few doors, but finding doctors to defend another doctor was usually not a problem unless the medical care was egregious, or the defendant doctor had a bad reputation within the medical community.

By the 1990s, there was no shortage of doctors willing to testify for a price. And the number of medical malpractice cases engulfed courthouses across the country. Given the high fees charged by experts-for-hire, intimidation tactics of opposing experts was off the game board. The money was too good. Out-of-state experts swooped in the night before they had to testify, collected thousands of dollars in fees, and then ran to catch a taxi to the airport to fly home.

As the business of testifying caught on, some experts had reviewed 200 or more cases and testified at depositions and appeared at trial more often than the attorneys who hired them.

Doctors who testify frequently are near impossible to cross-examine in the courtroom. Think of a buzzing mosquito trying to feed off a block of granite. Well-traveled experts see trap questions coming from a long way off. Their popularity has a lot to do with their expertise, and I don't mean in the practice of medicine.

In law school, I learned that trials in the American legal system rely on the adversary process to bring clarity to competing versions of the truth and to reveal a fair result. Ideally, we call this "justice." However, with the influx of expert witnesses for hire, cross-examination and the search for truth in the courtroom became an elusive target.

Of all the legal scholars, law books, and law professors, no one captured the "search for the truth" in a trial better than Jonathan Harr's *A Civil Action*, a nonfiction account (which was later adapted into a film) of plaintiff families of cancer-stricken children suing two companies for polluting the city's drinking water.

In a revealing scene in the movie, the two opposing lawyers sit on a bench outside the courtroom while the jury deliberates. The defense attorney's confidence has been tempered by how the evidence favors the plaintiff. The defense lawyer, played by Robert Duvall, is attempting to negotiate a settlement with the plaintiff's lawyer, played by John Travolta. Once the evidence is put to the jury and witnesses have either shined or stumbled terribly, lawyers can see verdict possibilities more clearly. In dramatic fashion, John Travolta refuses a reasonable offer of settlement and then declares that the jury will see the truth. The grizzled defense attorney, acting incredulous, says the courtroom is no place to find the truth.

In Harr's book, he accounts for the commonly misunderstood gap between the spirit of the law and the reality of the courtroom. He quotes a treatise on evidence written in 1905 by the prominent legal scholar John

Wigmore: "Cross-examination is beyond doubt the greatest legal engine ever invented for the discovery of truth. A lawyer can do anything with cross-examination. . . . He may, it is true, do more than he ought to do; he . . . may make the truth appear like a falsehood."

Beneath Wigmore's quote, Harr adds the words of Jerry Facher, the real-life defense counsel portrayed in the movie:

"The truth?" Facher said, smiling, one day after court. "The truth is at the bottom of a bottomless pit."

Although Wigmore published his treatise on evidence in 1905, the lines about truth in the courtroom have stuck with me even today. And I know of no better one-sentence summary of the reality of trial work than Facher's statement.

I had been introduced to gamesmanship in the prosecutor's office. But medical malpractice litigation plays out like a game of chess on a giant board. There are chess pieces representing medical evidence: doctors' and nurses' notes, lab data, test results, vital signs, X-rays, past medical records, medications, and any documentation of a patient's past medical problems. Medical experts are the power pieces. Experienced trial lawyers learn that intimidation, bias and prejudice, and other persuasive intangibles external to the rules governing the admission and exclusion of evidence often eclipse logic and reasoning. As I mentioned, hired experts are not intimidated. They pose one of the most challenging aspects of a medical malpractice trial. After decades of cross-examining hired guns, I still struggle with experts that say to the jury, "I'm here because I feel it's my responsibility to promote the best practices of medicine for patients." What I'd like to say is, "You're a windbag who has grabbed a few facts and are making the rest of the crap up. And you're good at it—that's why you're in the courtroom so often." I would like to make that accusation, but since I use experts who have testified frequently, that accusation would blow up in my face.

The defense hires medical experts, some just as expensive and experienced in the courtroom as their counterparts on the plaintiff's side. However, I have never had to use experts advertised for litigation purposes. We don't need to use physicians promoting their interest in the business of litigation, though we sometimes use experts that have testified just as frequently as plaintiff's experts and charge the same. The only time I have difficulty finding a doctor to serve as an expert is when the doctor, in good conscience, can't defend the decisions made by my client. Some defense medical experts have never testified against another physician and won't. Yet I know in many cases, despite a doctor providing good medical care, death or disability cannot be prevented. I learned that even as medicine advanced, many diseases are unforgiving and refractory to treatment. The death of a patient engenders sympathy. The result? Sympathy hangs over the courtroom like the blade of a guillotine, and even the most qualified expert is not enough to persuade a jury that the doctor did nothing wrong.

This is the adversarial process as I have experienced it both as a plaintiff's lawyer and later defending physicians. To the uninitiated, I may sound cynical and harsh, but it's the reality of high stakes litigation where lawyers are paid to win.

20 Comparative Law: The Evil Empire

Lesson 20: You know this already: our legal system is far from perfect, but the penal system is one of the best.

In America, we lawyers vigorously, or should I say zealously, protect the individual rights of our clients. Anything that unfairly prejudices our clients' right to a fair trial catapults a trial lawyer front and center in the courtroom. This is not the case everywhere in the world. In 1988, I traveled to the Soviet Union with 150 American citizens as part of the Chautauqua Institution and USSR Friendship Society, a people-to-people cultural, academic, and performing arts exchange. The historic Chautauqua Institution is a nonprofit educational arts, music, and non-denominational religious center founded in the 1870s. The flagship campus sits on the shores of Chautauqua Lake, in the southwest corner of the state of New York. I grew up ten miles from the Institution, caddied at its golf course during high school, and climbed over the iron-spiked fence surrounding the grounds on summer nights.

My interest in Russia, however, had more to do with midlife boredom with plaintiff's personal injury work than cultural curiosity. I wrote a check for $5,000 to the Bestor Society—a donation to Friends of the Chautauqua Institution—and I was on my way to the "Evil Empire," according to President Reagan.

In Moscow, we were immediately greeted by Soviet officials and Intourist functionaries—refrigerated personalities who said *nyet* to any request outside our predetermined schedule. Our itinerary included three days in Moscow, three days in St. Petersburg, and a weeklong conference in Tbilisi, Georgia, at the time one of the Soviet Socialist Republics.

If there were evil people in Russia—and I assume they have their share—I didn't recognize them. I had the distinct feeling, though, that we were being watched. Except for our official guides and gloom-faced overseers denying any request outside our official itinerary, we met Soviet citizens curious about America, envious of our freedom and opportunity, friendly, and, in many ways, sharing the same concerns about making ends meet and establishing a better life for their children. The younger generation spoke freely and seemed optimistic. Older citizens were more guarded.

It took all of one day to see that the standard of living in the Soviet Union had the markings of a third-world country. One morning, walking to a conference in Tbilisi, we had to hop-step around a large excavation that had taken out the entire sidewalk. We commented on the lack of any warning signs or barriers, and obviously no accountability.

Another lawyer and I wanted to see a Soviet courthouse. The Soviet guide assigned to us appeared stumped by our request. She disappeared, but returned an hour later with a car and driver. Off we went, feeling very official. This experience for me had more meaning than all the meetings, lectures, and official parties I attended. We drove around central Moscow for two hours in search of a courthouse. No luck. I had the brainy idea of asking a policeman for directions. In the USA, cops know the locations of the courthouses in their jurisdiction because they are routinely subpoenaed for trial. Soviet cops stared blankly in response to our questions.

Finally, we pulled up to a large, nondescript brick building that had the look of a warehouse. We entered through an unmarked single door facing a side street, then went up a narrow stairway leading to a courtroom with no jury box and no witness stand. Our guide disappeared, eventually returning with a woman she introduced as a judge. The judge didn't speak English. We couldn't speak Russian. Our questions (interpreted by our guide) about types of cases and trials were met with quizzical expressions. My questions about civil litigation and medical malpractice were either lost in translation, or maybe they were unspeakable transgressions of the Soviet system. The judge exhibited no interest in two American lawyers.

In stark contrast to this undignified structure, emblematic of the Soviet-run legal system, the architecture of American courthouses symbolizes the primacy and dominate force of the rule of law. Ohio's courthouses were built in the neoclassical style. Drive east from Columbus for about 50 miles on Route 161 and you'll reach Newark, the county seat of Licking County, named after the salt licks in the area. (If you're not from around this part of Ohio, Newark is pronounced "Nerk.") One of Ohio's many majestic courthouses sits smack in the middle of Newark's town square. Like many rural counties in Ohio, the town center is organized around the county courthouse. The Licking County courthouse is constructed of limestone in characteristic Second Empire architectural style. The edifice looms over the town, featuring Lady Justice perched on a large domed clock.

I've tried three cases in this courthouse. Each time I walk into the larger of the two courtrooms, I get a sense of history—a place where Clarence Darrow would have fought for "truth, justice, and the American way." In Newark, county residents know where to look for justice—even foreign visitors will recognize the image of the central role of law in America.

On my return to the USA, I wrote a short piece on a lawyer's perspective of the Soviet legal system for the Institution's newspaper. I can't remember what I reported, other than that safety standards were nonexistent. But the differences I recognized immediately between the two legal systems were the absence of personal rights and access to a framework of justice. Fall and break your leg in an unmarked crevice in a walkway in America and you may get a letter from three contingent fee lawyers offering a free consultation and free representation. For me, the essential difference was the *opportunity* for litigants to hold people in authority accountable. Other than criminal trials, I saw no legal machinery in the Soviet Union to hold the citizens or the Soviet state accountable.

In the United States, the right of free speech is enjoyed by both citizens and noncitizens. In Russia today, despite legal counsel, an outspoken Russian may get a free, all-expenses-paid, one-way trip to IK-3, a Soviet-era Gulag prison system just inside the Arctic Circle. I've complained about naïve jurors, inexperienced judges, and at times the long delays in judicial rulings. I can live with the occasional naive jury that doesn't follow the court's instructions becasue they don't fit the jury's view of how the world should work, and the influx of mediocre judges. But I can't tolerate the recent vindictiveness visited upon judges and lawyers because they take a position opposite that of governing authorities. That reminds me of the unmarked hole in the Tbilisi street and the lack of accountability.

21 Out of a Job

Lesson 21: The practice of law is both a profession and a business. To survive, businesses adjust to the changing times; lawyers must do the same.

In the early 1990s, the boom of lawyer TV commercials had begun sharing time with Ford, Chevy trucks, and the King of Beers. Lawyers pitching free consults began muscling in on my network of referring attorneys. Lawyers were on TV, radio, billboards, and the back covers of phone books. My referring lawyers in small towns like Marion, Chillicothe, and Marietta, Ohio, were losing clients to Cleveland and Columbus TV lawyers touting their toughness fighting insurance companies and getting the justice that you deserved. I tried placing a larger $500 advertisement in the Yellow Pages, but an effective half-page lawyer advertisement cost thousands. By my estimation, at that time the number of lawyers advertising for medical malpractice cases in the Yellow Pages nearly tripled.

But there was more to my empty cabinets than a puny advertisement in the Yellow Pages. The growing availability of expert witnesses for hire just a phone call away meant that finding experts suddenly became easy. Lawyers used to call me to discuss the merits of their claim and ask if I knew a doctor who might review their case. The old guard of med-mal lawyers like me weren't about to give up the names of experts we had worked so hard to cultivate. If I did, the lawyer wouldn't need me.

When the Columbus Bar Association first began advertising their lawyer referral program in central Ohio, I joined a list of four or five lawyers competent to handle medical malpractice referrals. By the early 1990s, more than 30 Columbus lawyers were signed up. In 1981, 24-hour music channel MTV played the catchy tune "Video Killed the Radio Star." By the end of the 1990s, except for a few well-regarded well-networked plaintiff's lawyers, TV lawyers killed attorney referrals and the new normal was that any patient ending up with a bad result after medical treatment meant something went wrong and somebody should pay.

In the middle of the drop-off in clients, I spent a year at Georgetown University Law Center. In November of 1992, after graduating and receiving my LLM in International Law, my dream of an appointment as an assistant secretary for the Department of Commerce crashed, along with George H. W. Bush's unsuccessful run for a second term. It was back to Columbus and the plaintiff's personal injury practice for me.

In my absence, my competitors missed few opportunities to spread the news that I had abandoned the plaintiff's practice. Rebuilding my practice in Columbus was slow going.

The thought of TV advertising was too embarrassing; trolling for clients between soap operas and game shows broke from my traditional thinking of the cherished image of the dignity of the legal profession. (And I should mention, I didn't have the money to hit the airwaves.)

By the 1990s, veteran malpractice defense attorneys switched sides and opened boutique plaintiff's firms. Former defense lawyers thought, "Why settle a case with a plaintiff's lawyer for $500,000 and get $20,000 in hourly fees, when you could collect 40 percent of a contingent fee for the same amount of work and get $200,000?" Advertising and the influx of converted defense lawyers began flooding the market with plaintiff's malpractice lawyers. Potential plaintiffs called the TV lawyer, not their local family attorney. Referrals dropped precipitously. By the year 2000, my phone went dead.

22 The Devil Inside

Lesson 22: Unfortunately, a trial lawyer's value to society is judged by the clients you represent.

I had an impressive résumé of trial experience, publications, and honored inductions to prestigious societies of outstanding trial lawyers. Just ask me. Yet, no one wanted me. Trial skills and reputation had carried me only so far. The ability to generate clients—the knack for getting business—is the difference between success and failure in any business, including the practice of law.

I hadn't done much on the lecture circuit after Georgetown and had tired of schmoozing referring lawyers (which I did half-heartedly anyway). I seldom felt comfortable asking lawyers for business. I've always hated sucking up, except to dreamboat.

I thought back to a trial in 1999. I'd finally won a medical malpractice trial against Gayle Arnold, one of the best defense trial attorneys in Ohio. Gayle had spanked me in two prior trials. Months after my "dog and pony show" (Gayle's description of my presentation to the jury), we flew to Chicago to take the deposition of my expert in another case. Traveling with opposing counsel is a common practice in our business. We were not the best of friends, but not enemies either. In the past Gayle and I had conversations about me joining his firm, but our conversation always ended with "you're too expensive." By 2001 my file cabinets were empty. I was a cheap hire.

Four months later, my name would be second on the letterhead: Arnold, Todaro, & Welch.

Before I abandoned the plaintiff's practice, I had cleaned out a storage unit where I retained all my closed files from the past 22 years. The empty feeling in my gut had nothing to do with shredding 200 files. As I sorted through pleadings, correspondence, and medical records, fractured images of my former clients appeared.

The moments were like watching home movies projected on a basement wall. The reality of the value of my legal services was disappointing. Essentially, I took money from an insurance company, put a doctor through hell, and split the money between me and my client. Maybe I made a significant difference in the quality of life of 50 of my 200 clients. The doctors I sued for negligence probably saved or improved the quality of life of 200 patients in one year—a humbling conclusion for any lawyer convinced that they possess a skill few others are capable of acquiring.

I thought of Brad Nunn, one of my close high school friends, with academic lowlights that equaled my own. He had become a superb high school principal. Later, working with troubled inner-city youth in Buffalo and Chicago, he had made a positive difference in more lives than me while living on a shrinking middle-class income. I earned good money as a plaintiff's lawyer, but except for a few clients, lawsuits accomplished little long-term difference in their lives.

Arnold, Todaro, & Welch's major client, ProAssurance, entered the Ohio medical malpractice insurance market in the late 1990s. A bitter wind soon followed. Plaintiff's lawyers affectionately called the insurance company "ProAss." ProAssurance was one of the rare insurance companies that refused to throw a few bucks at plaintiff's lawyers to encourage them to settle. They listened to their doctor clients and spent considerable energy determining whether the doctor's decisions were defensible in the courtroom.

My second week on the job, one of ProAssurance's roving troubleshooters discussed their business model with me. "First," he said, "we investigate and prepare our cases in the same way you did as a plaintiff's lawyer. If we get a negative review from a potential expert, we will look for another expert." (Geez, how did he know I did that?) "It's a mindset problem," he explained. "Many doctors willing to serve as expert witnesses are incapable of standing in the shoes of the defendant—to disengage from hindsight bias. Their ego will not allow them to see themselves making a decision that ultimately was the wrong decision.

"Second, our policies have consent clauses and no hammer clauses. Unlike most of the medical malpractice companies, ProAssurance gives the doctor ultimate authority over settlement of their case. It's also the reason that our policies are the most expensive in the market," the troubleshooter told me. "If the doctor refuses to settle, the plaintiffs have to go to trial or dismiss. Other insurance companies retain the exclusive right to settle despite the doctor's wishes, cutting litigation costs."

Not surprisingly, ProAssurance's business model reduced the number of lawsuits with marginal or nonexistent merit. "Our insured doctors," he instructed, "don't get a call from their lawyer on the eve of trial saying, 'It's too risky to take your case to trial, so we should pay half a million to avoid the possibility of a million-dollar verdict.'" And he made it clear ProAssurance didn't offer "nuisance settlements"—an offer of cash less than the cost of defending the case. "It may be cheaper to pay $50,000 to the plaintiff than pay our lawyers and experts a total of $100,000 to defend the case at trial, but that is not what we do at this company." I got it, but I knew this meant I would try a lot more cases.

This policy was an effective marketing tool for doctors worried their reputation would be thrown under the bus for expediency's sake. Since doctors usually believe they did the best they could under the circumstances, consent clauses forced more cases to trial.

Representing ProAssurance doctors had a downside: the wrath of our brethren on the bench. Judges spewed a river of fire when I refused to offer defense costs to plaintiffs eager to take a small settlement that would also rid the judge of a case on an overcrowded docket. No offer on the eve of trial forced the plaintiff's lawyer to try a case that they were unlikely to win, or to dismiss the case and eat the cost. ProAssurance's business model forced plaintiff's lawyers to choose their cases wisely.

I didn't have to guess what former colleagues on the plaintiff's side said about me. My brother called me within a month of my conversion to the "dark side." "Toady," he said, "I saw a poster at the courthouse with your name on it: 'Wanted: Dead or Alive' . . . with 'Alive' crossed out."

I got a call from my old boss, Dan Higgins, about a case he had against one of my clients. My doctor-client refused to consent to even a small amount, $25,000. Dan needed the money to pay off his litigation costs and give the rest to his client. He wanted nothing for himself. "When you work for the devil, you are the devil," he said, and he meant it.

My old pal Scott, who could find humor in a dumpster, called and started our conversation by humming the Charlie Daniels tune "The Devil Went Down to Georgia."

But the one that bothered me, just a little, came from a converted defense lawyer who had become a respected plaintiff's lawyer in Dayton. We stood outside the judge's chambers on the second floor of the historic courthouse in Springfield, Ohio, waiting to meet with the judge to discuss a trial date. The lawyer, in his 50s, wearing a navy blue suit with a paisley burgundy tie and matching pocket square, walked up to me and shook my hand.

Poker-faced, he said, "I've talked to lawyers in Columbus. They say you're a snake and not to be trusted, but I think I can work with you." At first, I thought he was kidding. He wasn't. I'd been a defense lawyer for one year.

When I joined the defense bar, representing doctors and insurance companies, I assumed my fellow plaintiff's lawyers would continue to appreciate my insight into medical conditions and medical malpractice. For years, my friends at the plaintiff's bar brainstormed their cases with me, and for some trusted friends I shared hard-to-find doctors who were willing to testify against another physician. What startled me was my near instantaneous transfiguration. I underestimated the deep distain plaintiff's lawyers have for someone taking food off their table. Because of the clash of financial incentives, I was reviled by the lawyers who for years had respected me and sought my counsel. The business and transactional lawyers I know mostly help their clients and work with opposing counsel to achieve a reasonably fair result. Trial lawyers ruffle feathers. Half of the time they do things to people, not for people.

A few years back, I had a T-shirt printed that announced, "I'm an honest lawyer, but $20 is $20." My wife often reminds me, "Not everyone thinks you're funny."

I remember sitting on our back porch at home, talking with Barb. "How did I become an evil son of a bitch . . . overnight?"

23 The Trickery of Hindsight

Lesson 23: Understand how the illusory wisdom of hindsight bias plays out in the courtroom.

As a plaintiff's lawyer suing doctors for 20 years, I had perfected hindsight analysis. I got good at it. My knowledge of the end result allowed me to use hindsight to pick a few facts from a cluster of medical data and connect the dots that led to the appearance of an obvious diagnosis.

First, I researched the disease. What are the typical complaints voiced by the patient? What are all the signs and symptoms, such as chest pain or shortness of breath? I learned how the doctor prioritizes the possible diagnoses—a mental checklist physicians call a differential diagnosis. What lab tests and imaging studies are supposed to be ordered? I would list the possible diagnoses and plot where the missed diagnosis fit in the lineup of possible diagnoses. I would read medical textbooks to learn what the best treatment was for a good result, and what happens to patients when necessary treatment is delayed..

Once I knew the medicine and best practices, I reviewed the patient's medical chart and made a list of every sign, symptom, and test result that was a positive finding associated with the disease or medical condition that killed or injured the plaintiff.

When cross-examining a defendant doctor, I asked questions that confirmed each positive item I found on the medical chart that was on the list of symptoms consistent with the delayed or missed diagnosis. As each sign or symptom piled up, the drumbeat of the diagnosis got louder and louder and insinuated that only a moron could have failed to see the red flags warning of an impending lethal condition.

This questioning technique simplifies a complex mental process. However, this cognitive trick is misleading in its oversimplification of how doctors make a diagnosis. Hindsight analysis makes us think we are smarter than we are. It gives us wisdom that the doctor could never have not knowing the outcome.

Hindsight eliminates the in-the-moment guesswork of sorting through signs and symptoms that suggest myriad illnesses. Hindsight's cognitive trick involves isolating and sequencing cherry-picked medical facts that set up a logical conclusion. A few facts anchor the diagnosis, and now previous nonspecific facts (symptoms that do not clearly point to a cause or diagnosis) snowball into an obvious diagnosis.

Here is a typical example that probably happens daily in the practice of medicine. Sam is a 55-year-old man who works as a lineman for the city of Tucson. It's a hot July day and his stomach feels like he ate something bad. After work, he stops at an urgent care facility and tells the doctor he has indigestion, nausea, and felt lightheaded off and on. He mentions that his dad had a heart attack at about his age. The doctor thinks the heat and dehydration are responsible for his symptoms, and sends him home with instructions to follow up with his family doctor. Sam has a heart attack and dies two days later.

The doctor, however, does not have the benefit of knowing that Sam will have a heart attack, so she cannot know whether feeling lightheaded is caused by an impending heart attack or a smorgasbord of other more common maladies. She must consider all the nonspecific signs and symptoms: dehydration on a hot day, vertigo, and/or low blood sugar possibly causing lightheadedness. Then, she must sort through a cluster of complaints, signs, and symptoms and decide the most likely diagnosis. It's difficult for her to connect the dots.

In Sam's medical case, his symptoms were consistent with a heart attack, but were *more likely* consistent with less life-threatening conditions. On his physical examination, he did not have chest pain, substernal pain, or shortness of breath—automatic triggers for the doctor to order an EKG. He wasn't a smoker or overweight, and didn't lead a sedentary life. These factors figured most prominently in the doctor's mind with the information she had *at the time*.

Yet, once we know that Sam died from a heart attack, that knowledge allows a lawyer to work backward and give more weight to the symptoms of nausea, indigestion, and lightheadedness—common symptoms of an individual having a heart attack. Now the lawyer can isolate and emphasize these symptoms so that a juror can visualize the heart attack coming. Now it was very predictable. Hindsight makes the jurors smarter than the doctor.

This type of thinking is what cognitive psychologists call *hindsight bias*. This mindset overestimates and speeds up the time in which individuals can predict the bad result. As a plaintiff's attorney, this technique served me well. Now, on the defense side, I saw hindsight bias as a form of deception. Behavior psychologists have studied hindsight bias and report that it's more illusory than real, and a defect of mental cognition. I had to learn how to deconstruct the predictable and inevitable diagnosis of an impending heart attack in lawsuits like Sam's, or there would be no justice for my clients.

Daily, doctors must expeditiously make medical decisions based on imperfect tests and incomplete data. And sometimes they are wrong, but they're not negligent.

The human condition fails to realize we are not as smart as we think we are. Hindsight is not wisdom. Yes, we learn from hindsight. But hindsight makes us think we knew it all along. Navigating uncertainty in medicine is like attempting to assemble a jigsaw puzzle without the photo on the box cover. And the doctor is under time constraints. Yet once we use hindsight to figure out the mistake made, we suddenly are so much smarter than the doctor who didn't figure things out sooner.

24 The Most Important Doctor You've Never Met

Lesson 24: We can learn a lot from radiologists about why we make mistakes. It's not a lack of intelligence or incompetence. It's the failure to continually remind ourselves that our brain automatically takes shortcuts to make sense of the world, and shortcuts miss important information.

Carl finished emailing his plant supervisors in Toledo and Grand Rapids instructions on plastic container shipments to Amsterdam. It was a gray, overcast November morning in Columbus. After breakfast, Carl loaded his kids and backpacks onto his golf cart and drove down to the edge of the driveway and waited for the school bus. Twenty minutes later, Carl died taking a shower.

Carl was a big man, but not obese. He didn't smoke, and only drank socially. He was active, played golf, and was otherwise healthy, except for a hospitalization five years ago for DVTs—blood clots in the deep veins in his legs. DVT is a medical abbreviation for deep vein thrombosis. Carl's doctors had inserted a filter in the inferior vena cava, a large vein that transports deoxygenated blood from all parts of the body to the heart. The filter catches clots and prevents them from obstructing the flow of blood to the lungs, causing back pressure on the heart, and without warning, the heart could stop beating.

The day before Carl died, he had gone to the emergency room at a nearby hospital complaining of abdominal pain. Carl didn't complain of chest pain or shortness of breath, symptoms that would warn of a heart issue or blood clots blocking blood flow to the lungs. There are a multitude of medical possibilities that could cause abdominal pain, so the emergency room doctor ordered an abdominal CT (computed tomography) with contrast to look for any medical abnormality causing abdominal pain. This imaging study is done with dye to highlight the anatomy and if, for example, the dye doesn't fill the veins that drain from the liver into the vena cava, the patient may have clots impeding flow. The radiologist on duty that day was Neil Jeffers. He interpreted Carl's CT. He concluded there were no abnormalities seen on the CT. Carl was sent home with the usual instructions to follow up with his family doctor if the symptoms continued.

Carl was 41 years old. He and his wife had two children. His wife would show the jury his yearly W2s exceeding $750,000. She sued the radiologist after Carl's death and her lawyers turned down a million-dollar settlement and instead would ask the jury for $10 million.

Dr. Jeffers did his best work in the dark. I'm not talking about a party boy late Saturday night; I am talking about a doctor sitting in a dark room, with no windows, no distractions, intently focused on monitors displaying digital images of body parts, such as the brain or spine. Radiologists scrutinize black and white images separated by 250 shades of gray at 5- to 12-minute intervals, ranging from 10,000 to 15,000 cases a year. Neil rarely meets his patients. He doesn't have the opportunity to ask "What brings you in today?", or take a history of past medical problems, or perform physical examinations, or order lab tests. In a moment's time, radiologists must recognize abnormal anatomy and know its cause. Here lies a tricky curve with no bright yellow line marking the wrong side of the road. Eighty to 90 percent of the imaging studies read daily by a radiologist are either normal or show typical variations of normal anatomy. Unfortunately, outcome bias—judging the quality of a decision based on the (bad) result—is a recurring assault on the practice of radiology.

The first radiology case I defended involved a delay in diagnosis of breast cancer. The plaintiffs had circled a couple of whitish specks and drawn arrows pointing to them on a mammogram. They claimed the specks were a cluster of calcifications, highly suspicious of breast cancer. The plaintiff's tumor was diagnosed in the same area of the calcifications.

The plaintiff's lawyer would show the jury radiology films annotated with circles and arrows highlighted in red—the subtle evidence of cancer. My client, though, said the pattern of calcifications was nothing unusual and he had seen this constellation of calcifications before, and they were not suspicious of cancer, nor did they turn out to be cancer. But the plaintiff's radiology expert saw a worrisome pattern of calcifications. The calcifications had to be suspicious, because he knew from later mammograms that they *were* cancerous lesions.

Defending radiologists opened a window into the science of human error. No other medical specialist struggles for diagnostic clarity in a shorter time span than the lonely radiologist. After four decades of medical malpractice litigation and a year at Ohio State University School of Medicine, I know of no other medical specialist more vulnerable to the cottage industry of medical malpractice lawsuits than radiologists. Emergency room doctors are a close second.

Greg Foliano, my partner, recently hired because of his unusual ability to grasp complex medical concepts and paint plaintiff's medical experts into a corner, had asked me to help him defend Dr. Jeffers' case. I met Neil in the lobby of our office on a warm spring day. "Hi Doc," I said, extending my hand. "I'm Jerry Todaro."

"I wish I could say I'm glad to meet you," he said. I laughed. He didn't. The fingers on his right hand were two degrees south of frostbite. Neil was a tall, lanky man in his late 40s. He had a round face and a buzz cut. His horn-rimmed glasses gave him a nerdy look. When we sat down in our medical library to review the CT scans, Neil kept crossing and uncrossing his legs. I was scrolling the images of the CT on the computer when Neil grabbed my arm. "Hey, am I going to lose my house?" His face was etched with anguish.

"Nope," I said, "you won't lose your house," but I gave no other explanation. Whether we would win or not I didn't know.

Researchers in the practice of radiology have published articles and book chapters on the "limitations of biologic and physiologic perception," also known as "the human limits of visual acuity." Despite technological advancements from the days of looking at a single X-ray on a view box to a single MRI with 500 digital frames, the error rate for radiologists over the past 50 years has remained a consistent 2 to 4 percent. Imaging studies remain an imperfect tool, and the mind's eye has its inherent limitations. The question in radiology is when does "uncertainty end, and interpreter error begin," according to Michael Bruno, MD, author of *Error and Uncertainty in Diagnostic Radiology*. I would add: When does unavoidable error end and negligence begin?

Because of my reading of the medical literature, I had cobbled together a defense for situations where the radiologist is given an "inadequate history," and the test ordered is not the best test to discover the abnormality.

I can't recall the authors and citations, but here is how the wrong reason given by the doctor ordering a CT scan affects a radiologist interpretation. Despite years of training, radiologists, like all of us, suffer from limitations of human visual perception. This limitation is confounded by the patient's history or the reason for ordering an MRI or any other imaging study. The patient's background history—a fall or sudden headache—is so important to the radiologist because it drives expectations and increases the doctor's perception and focus. An emergency room doctor evaluating an elderly patient who fell and hit her head, for example, will order a head CT looking for blood on the brain. The zone of interest or high-yield area focuses on searching for evidence of blood on the brain. However, if, for example, this same patient has a noncancerous cyst deep in their brain tissue and a low-yield area for bleeding caused by a knock on the head, an MRI would be more sensitive than a CT scan. The combination of an inferior imaging study, an incomplete history, and the inherent limits of visual acuity often cause the radiologist to miss the presence of a cyst. In Neil's defense, our job was to educate jurors to understand and accept that mistaken observations are an unavoidable element of the human condition, and sometimes no matter how hard a radiologist tries, he cannot avoid making mistakes. The challenge for us was getting jurors to see the line separating mistakes caused by the limits of human performance rather than negligence.

Carl's lawyers claimed that a log jam of clots had formed just below the filter in his inferior vena cava. The clots had enlarged the inferior vena cava and veins emptying into the vena cava. The autopsy confirmed a massive number of clots had blocked vessels to the lungs, stopping the heart. When Neil and I met at our first meeting, we reviewed the film he had interpreted the day before Carl died. I asked him, "Do you see clots in the inferior vena cava?"

"No," he said, shaking his head, "there's nothing here, and a standard CT with contrast is not the best way to look inside the vena cava." A CT with contrast injects dye into the veins to better visualize the abnormalities of body organs and structures. The dye, Neil pointed out, had not had enough time to flow down to the vena cava.

The plaintiff's radiology expert disagreed. "Clots," he said, "had filled the vena cava, the diameter of the vena cava was larger than normal, and the veins leading to the vena cava were bigger, too."

In my mind, I had already reviewed the checklist of defenses that resonate with the average human being, whether a parent, a supervisor, or an athlete. Any activity that requires a combination of mental activity and visual detection, at some point, humbles all of us. Radiologists have studied erroneous conclusions in diagnostic radiology and have categorized several common mental mistakes. My strategy was to place the jury in the shoes of the radiologist, without actually asking them to do that. Rules of trial practice do not allow lawyers to ask a juror to put themselves in the position of the plaintiff or defendant. The jury must make judgments based on what a reasonable person would do. (Note to any law students reading along: Contrary to the instructions jurors receive before deliberation, jurors make decisions from their gut—what would *I do*, what *do I expect*.)

Research in radiology cites common cognitive failures, some of them well understood by any juror. For example, when an abnormality is first seen, it is believed to be more serious than it is. An enlarged lymph node is not normal, but may be mistakenly believed to be cancerous because of its size. This is an example of a false positive. In a business setting, a false positive is like hiring an employee with great credentials, but the employer fails to evaluate the employee's divisive personal skills. Radiologists attribute this error to "complacency."

Another common error that is not exclusive to radiologist is "poor communication": an abnormality is identified and interpreted correctly, but the message does not reach the clinician. Occasionally, a radiologist identifies a life-threatening bulging aneurism, but only puts it in her report and never calls the ordering emergency room doctor. Unfortunately, the failure to initiate early warnings has also claimed many lives from catastrophic tornados, flooding, and fast-moving fire storms.

Another cognitive error classification that was of no help in defending Neil is one of the more common mistakes that radiologists call "satisfaction of search." Here, once an abnormality is identified, "other abnormalities on an image are missed . . . because of the failure to continue to search for additional abnormalities after the first was found, according to Dr. Bruno.[1] The radiologist becomes satisfied after finding the first abnormality and quits the interpretation process. Cognitive psychologists have studied real-world scenarios in what they call "visual search distractions" involving multiple target searches; for example airport security screenings for contraband items. For prosecutors, this lapse plays out when the police arrest one suspect and fail to continue their investigation, and the real culprit evades arrest.

On that day Neil and I first met, we sat in front of the oversized monitor in our medical library pondering the plaintiff's expert opinions. Neil explained why the CT of the abdomen ordered in this case, with omnipaque contrast, was not the optimal study to find blood clots in the vena cava. This imaging study takes a snapshot of the liver 70 seconds after the contrast is injected. The purpose of this study is to allow radiologists to visualize the tissue of the *liver* and to find defects such as cysts and tumors. Neil explained that the venous blood with opaque dye did not have enough time to flow through the venous system down the legs and back up to the inferior vena cava just below the heart. The lack of dye was not the result of obstruction from blood clots, but the result of shooting the image of the liver at 70 seconds instead of two minutes later. The protocol for a venogram, the best study to look for blood clots in the inferior vena cava, Neil said, calls for timing the snapshot of the liver at 120 to 150 seconds after injection of the contrast. This allows the dye to reach the liver and the vena cava. Greg had previously explained our defense. This imaging study fell into the category of not the *best* study. Researchers have identified "test limitations" as a significant cause of missed findings.

Besides dealing with hindsight and outcome bias, one of Neil's colleagues stuck his nose where it didn't belong. Doug Richter (a radiologist in the same group as Neil) and the plaintiff's lawyer belonged to the same golf club. When Dr. Richter heard about Carl's death, he accessed Carl's imaging studies at the hospital. Then, according to the plaintiff's lawyer, Richter told the golf pro that Neil missed a pulmonary embolus. Of course, plaintiff's counsel demanded Dr. Richter's deposition.

I could see this scenario unfold in the courtroom. What I would do if I was suing the radiologist? I'd say the defense was trying to cover up a mistake, but even the defendant's own colleagues were willing to tell the truth. I'd say, "Defense counsel, ladies and gentlemen, wants you to

1. Michael Bruno, MD, Error and Uncertainty in Diagnostic Radiology (2018).

believe that this log jam of clots in the vena cava was too subtle to see, yet the defendant's own partner reviewed the films and saw the clots, and he believes it was a mistake not to see them."

Later in the case, Dr. Richter was deposed and denied saying there were obvious clots in the inferior vena cava. To counter Dr. Richter's testimony, the plaintiffs argued that Richter's statements to the golf pro was an admission against interest—a rule of evidence that allows a jury to listen to hearsay evidence of a co-employee to third persons, because people don't make statements against their own well-being or contradict the employer's business practices unless they are true. Since the radiology group was a defendant, the plaintiffs claimed that Dr. Richter's statement that "Neil missed it" was admissible against the radiology group and Neil, despite what Dr. Richter said in his deposition.

So our only chess move here was to exclude Dr. Richter's statements to the golf pro because it didn't fit the admission against interest hearsay exception. Dr. Richter was not in the scope of his employment (which is a necessary foundation to assert this rule) when nosing around medical records of Carl in violation of HIPAA's privacy restrictions. Besides, Richter knew what happened, and he admitted he looked at the CT scan seven times.

As trial neared, we discussed the possibility of settling out of court. Neil understood he was victimized by outcome bias. We explained our fear that our defense was too technical for the jury to follow. He gave us his consent to settle the case and avoid a trial. We offered seven figures to settle.

"No way," was the plaintiff's response. They wanted $4 million or they were going to try the case.

The hospital's lawyers thought better of going to trial and wanted out. They paid a handsome sum to bail out of the courtroom.

Excluding Dr. Richter's damning statements depended on the trial judge agreeing with us that Richter's statements did not fit the hearsay exception of an admission against interest. The trial judge agreed with us. The plaintiff's attorney argued vociferously, at times railing at the judge, waving his arms in disbelief, but this diminutive, steely-eyed female judge never blinked. We liked our judge; she was decisive and controlled her courtroom. (In full disclosure, I have to say, I have never met a judge I didn't like that ruled in my favor.)

When the plaintiffs rested their case, we still felt we had a fighting chance. We had hired a highly credentialed radiology expert. Richard

Baron was the chairman of the Department of Radiology at the University of Chicago. He had board positions and leadership roles in the Radiology Society of America, the American College of Radiology, and hundreds of publications in major medical journals, but his most influential credential was his appointment as an examiner for the American Board of Radiology. In short, he tested young doctors taking the examination to become board certified in radiology, and he didn't disappoint.

What made him special was his gift of humanizing the mistakes of radiologists to a level of the everyday mental errors and misadventures of an average person. Two of the factors he used to evaluate radiologists were the reason for ordering X-rays and the technical parameters of the imaging study. When he addressed Neil's interpretation, he explained that inadequate history and an inferior imaging study degrades human visual perception. Carl's history on the radiology request said abdominal pain, not chest pain. Chest pain would have clued the radiologist to look for causes of chest pain, like pulmonary embolism. The best imaging study to order for visualization of the inferior vena cava is a venogram, which allows the dye up to three minutes to get to the inferior vena cava. The CT ordered by the emergency room doctor was a portal venous phase study, a scan that snaps a picture of the liver, which includes the inferior vena cava before the dye gets there. The jury found in favor of Neil after two hours, which is very fast for a complicated case.

The plaintiff appealed the verdict, arguing that excluding Dr. Richter's testimony was an error. The appellate court reversed the trial judge's decision to exclude the golf pro from telling the jury what Dr. Richter told him.

I met with Neil after the appellate court's decision. Given the jury's quick verdict, we didn't think that the golf pro's testimony about what Dr. Richter said would make a difference in the next trial. The jury understood that a portal venous phase study would not show clots even if they were there, and it was not fair to declare Neil negligent. But Neil told me he was done with the courtroom. He did not want to go back. The stress was too much.

We settled rather than retry Neil's case. I didn't know until after we settled that the plaintiff's lawyer talked to the jury, and they were not persuaded by the opinion that an enlarged vena cava and vessels were abnormal findings.

There are a lot of takeaways from defending radiologists. Cognitive mental errors are not the stuff of malpractice. Lack of intellect is not the problem. Training the mind is the cure for cognitive deficiencies. Yet, what I've learned from radiologists is our brains control what we see and hear.

In lawsuits involving medical testimony, juries have struggled with understanding the uncertainty of the predictability of human responses to both the natural course of diseases and their treatment. Our values, no matter how misguided, filter facts and opinions—sometimes leaving hard, persuasive facts powerless; hence the ease with which people use hindsight and outcome bias to fill gaps in knowledge and understanding. That's why lawyers find it nearly impossible to change the mind of a juror holding extreme beliefs. Information that does not confirm or match what they value does not change how they see the world. During jury selection, lawyers try to excavate, mostly unsuccessfully, preexisting mindsets that automatically reject their version of reality. Core values and hindsight form a brick wall in the courtroom.

Medicine depends a lot on science, and there are many among us that see medical science as snake oil. I don't have the ability to inspire a juror or anyone else to silence their core beliefs during a two-week trial. Do we have the best legal system in the world? On paper, yes; but as my friend Fagan said, the problem with justice is not the law, it's the people.

25 The Art of Gamesmanship

Lesson 25: No matter how much evidence, science, and logic you throw at a jury, they rely substantially on their gut reactions.

The cold, lifeless body lying naked on a stainless steel surgical table had died less than an hour after complaining of severe chest pain. The blade of the scalpel cut a bloodless Y-shaped incision from the shoulders, joining at the sternum. The junior medical resident then ran a single midline incision down to the man's pubic bone. Even a doctor-in-training knew what to look for: atherosclerotic plaque shutting down the heart's major coronary artery, a condition doctors often call "the widow-maker." Emergency room medical records accompanying the body left little doubt: a heart attack killed this man.

Days before, Phil Long had walked out of the bathroom, clutching his chest; perspiration dripped from his forehead. He told his wife, "Marcia, this is it. I'm not going to make it."

Paramedics arrived. Strong painkillers and nitroglycerine—a drug that dilates coronary arteries—did nothing to relieve his chest pain. EMS rushed him to the nearest emergency room. Nurses immediately hooked him up to a 12-lead EKG. To the untrained eye, the heart rhythms danced wildly on the monitor. What the ER nurse saw was ventricular fibrillation. The grim reaper peered over her shoulder. The pace in the ER quickened. Phil Long's heart conduction system—the electrical activation sequence of the heart's four pumping chambers—was out of sync. When the heart fibrillates, the heart quivers instead of pumping blood.

Unless the doctors act quickly, using a defibrillator to restore normal rhythm, filling out a death certificate is the next order of business.

According to the emergency room records, despite doctors and nurses administering powerful heart stimulants and three electrical shocks, the beeping sound on the heart monitor slowly dropped to 50 beeps, then 40, then 20, then a continuous blare—the electronic sound of death. Thirty-two minutes after he'd been wheeled into the ER, the code team suspended life-saving efforts.

When Phil's wife arrived at the hospital, a priest met her at the entrance of the emergency room. He took her to the ER bay where her husband lay motionless. A catheter in his arm snaked up to a plastic bag of clear solution hanging from an IV pole. An endotracheal tube protruded from the corner of his mouth. EKG lead wires dangled from his bare chest. The screen on the heart monitor was black and silent.

Marcia started screaming. Between gasping sobs, she kept asking, "Why, why? He was just in here in November. Why did this happen?" Four months ago, he'd been treated at the same hospital for a small stroke. Doctors, including a cardiologist, had evaluated him for seven days. They never said anything about a bad heart.

On the day of the autopsy, Dr. Janes, a full professor in the department of pathology at OSU's School of Medicine, supervised a second-year pathology resident. The death was no mystery: a 58-year-old man with high blood pressure, diabetes, obesity, high cholesterol, and a recent stroke—a cardiac train wreck waiting to happen.

Weeks later, peering through his microscope at the samples taken from Phil Long's coronary arteries, what caught Dr. Janes' attention was the narrowing of the left anterior descending artery, the LAD. The LAD is the most important of the three major arteries that supplies blood to the muscle of the left ventricle, the largest pumping chamber of the heart. If plaque buildup inside the first segment of the LAD pathway chokes off blood flow, the lack of blood flow causes the heart's conduction system to beat erratically and stop. Dr. Janes estimated an 80 percent buildup of plaque inside the LAD. He concluded that severe atherosclerosis of the LAD led to sudden cardiac arrest.

Mrs. Long called a lawyer.

Phil Long had suffered a stroke four months before his death because a clot blocked an artery in his brain. When Phil was hospitalized, one of his attending doctors had asked Dr. Amit Rafi to evaluate whether the arterial clot in his brain came from his heart, a common cause of strokes. Amit spent 30 minutes evaluating Phil and cleared him for the imaging study to look at his heart. The three-page consult note stated: "Recent onset of chest pain and shortness of breath . . . because of his risk factors and chest discomfort, *an eventual thallium stress test will be needed to rule out coronary artery disease.*" SMOKING GUN might as well have been stamped on the front page of the consult.

Dr. Rafi immediately dictated a consultation note into the hospital's internal transcription system. The consult note floated in the transcript queue, and never forwarded on to Phil's rehab chart. As Phil recovered from the stroke, his rehab doctors were unaware of the recommendation for a stress test.

In his opening statement at trial, Mrs. Long's lawyer would waive the consult note back and forth like a flagman at a railroad crossing. The jury's eyes shifted to Amit when the plaintiff's lawyer pointed at Dr. Rafi. "Philip Long died because the defendant failed to tell any of Phil's treating doctors that Phil needed a stress test."

My partner, John Welch, feared the captivating simplicity of the plaintiff's argument. Mr. Long needed a stress test; Amit Rafi never told Phil, his wife, or his treating doctors that Phil needed a cardiac stress test; according to the coroner, Phil died from a clogged coronary artery; a cardiac stress test would have discovered the clot. The logical conclusion was that a routine stress test and stent to open the LAD would have saved Phil's life. "If only Dr. Rafi had told Phil at bedside he needed a stress test, we wouldn't be in this courtroom today," Mrs. Long's lawyer would repeatedly remind the jury.

Before the trial started, the lawyers for the hospital employees thought it wise to settle, rather than attempt to explain that sometimes consult notes fall through the cracks. But Amit Rafi didn't believe he'd done anything wrong. He had completed an accelerated college and medical school program at Indiana University and graduated from Kreck School of Medicine in just six years. At the age of 31, he had earned board certifications in internal medicine, cardiology, and interventional cardiology. The respect he had earned in the hospital, with referring doctors, with patients, and with his family now hung over an abyss. His reputation was at stake. He wanted to fight. Amit was furious; he had told Phil he needed a stress test, and the coroner, according to Amit, was wrong, regardless of his credentials.

Because there was no documentation of the discussion, the plaintiff's lawyer would insinuate that Dr. Rafi was lying and was refusing to take responsibility for his mistake.

John Welch studied the medical literature that explained the pathophysiology of heart attacks. Years of medical research had shown that 90 percent of the time, sudden cardiac arrest results from *plaque rupture* and resulting *thrombus formation*. When plaque inside the wall of the coronary artery breaks off, a blood clot forms at the site of the break. The clot formation is called "thrombosis." A large thrombus can choke off the blood supply to the heart. It's as if a tractor-trailer jackknifes on an interstate, blocking all southbound lanes.

Dr. Janes hadn't found a thrombus in the LAD, only plaque—so no plaque rupture and no clot. Dr. Janes concluded that the plaque itself had narrowed the interior space of the LAD by 80 percent—as if one of the lanes on the interstate remained partially open, but not wide enough for cars to pass safely. We would argue to the jury that Dr. Janes' findings and his opinion didn't add up.

The difference was crucial to Dr. Rafi's defense. Plaque gradually narrowing a coronary artery often caused warning symptoms: chest pain, shortness of breath, and fatigue. But a thrombus completely obstructing the LAD commonly causes the immediate loss of heart function. If, as we asserted in Dr. Rafi's defense, a partial buildup without evidence of rupture or thrombus in the LAD usually doesn't cause sudden death, then something else went wrong in Phil's heart. And if the plaque identified by the coroner hadn't killed Mr. Long, then inserting a stent in the site of the narrowed LAD would not have prevented the unidentified heart problem that killed him.[1]

This was not the first time one of our doctors had been sued because of what we believed was an erroneous medical conclusion by a coroner. In this case, we needed to show the jury that plaque buildup doesn't cause a patient to die in a few minutes. Despite the coroner's opinion, our expert would argue it was far more probable that Philip Long's enlarged heart stopped from a sudden shower of tiny clots. These clots were unrelated to the stable plaque in the LAD.

1. You may be starting to find this medical information confusing. Now imagine explaining it to a jury and making it sound more compelling than "The coroner made a mistake."

Dr. Rafi wanted us to send published medical research explaining the different consequences of stable versus unstable plaque to the plaintiff's attorney and his experts. "Surely they will change their opinion," he said, frustrated.

"Trust me on this," I told him. "The plaintiffs hired Dr. Janes and another well-traveled expert witness to testify that YOU caused Philip Long's death. They will not change their opinions no matter what we put in front of them: not medical literature, not medical records, not the King James Bible. Once plaintiff's experts agree to testify at trial, they champion the plaintiff's cause—a paid pitchman for the plaintiff on the witness stand." Of course, the plaintiff's counsel didn't think much of our experts, either. In full disclosure, we expect the same from the expert witnesses we hire.

Experts rarely lie outright on the witness stand, but some hired guns shamelessly select one or two medical facts supporting their opinion while ignoring other, more compelling information that logically undermines their conclusion. Again, in the immortal words of Frank Ray, they "tell the truth attractively."

Experienced trial lawyers know that more times than not, drafting precise questions and then trapping the hired gun into conceding their version of the truth is a fantasy fostered by watching too many *Boston Legal* reruns. Seasoned expert witnesses see the big picture in the courtroom—the giant chessboard of medical facts. A few of these experts won't concede an argument that contradicts the theories they've pitched to the jury, no matter how unreasonable their explanations.

What makes cross-examination of seasoned medical experts so difficult? Trial lawyers like to say it's like taking a knife to a gunfight. We play in the doctors' ballpark, and they are intelligent. Physician experts who have testified in depositions and trials 50 times or more are as close to a colonoscopy in the courtroom as trial lawyers get. By this time in my career, I had learned that effective questioning of bright medical experts required attacking the assumptions supporting the expert's opinions, especially where critical facts supporting the expert's theory were absent. However, one damaging answer to a poorly framed open-ended question can send a lawyer slinking back to the counsel table with a harpoon in the chest.

In many, many cases, gamesmanship—not hard medical facts—drives tactics and strategy. Truly, Dr. Rafi's trial was a casebook study on gamesmanship in the courtroom. Tyler March, the lawyer for Mr. Long's estate, needed a cardiac pathologist to counter Dr. Rafi's opinion that the true diameter of the narrowed space inside the artery can't be determined on the autopsy table.

In a living person, arteries expand and contract under the constant pressure of the heart's pumping action. In death, arteries collapse like an unused, deflated fire hose. In Dr. Rafi's opinion, cardiac catheterization when Mr. Long was alive would not have shown dangerous narrowing of the LAD. If the jury accepted Amit's opinion, there was no medical indication for stent placement before Mr. Long died. There had to be another reason for Phil's heart attack.

Mr. March, a cagey plaintiff's lawyer deft at employing gambits on the medical chessboard, sensed weakness in his theory of the cause of Mr. Long's death. Like any good chess player, he searched for a powerful chess piece to counter Dr. Rafi's opinion. He found Dr. Guinn, a former professor of pathology at a Harvard teaching hospital who was associated with an expert witness service.

A major problem for one side of a case is having too many experts. The risk is conflicting opinions. To our great surprise, Dr. Guinn contradicted Dr. Janes. Dr. Guinn believed Mr. Long did have a clot in the LAD that was missed at the autopsy. Dr. Guinn would testify that the resident performing the autopsy failed to see the plaque rupture and clot because the sectioning of the coronary arteries was too far apart. The resident cut sections of the artery at 5-millimeter lengths instead of 1 or 2 millimeters.

John Welch searched for our own cardiac pathologist to back up Dr. Rafi's theory and rebut Dr. Guinn. John, a member of the prestigious American College of Trial Lawyers and a master strategist, hired Dr. James Mann to review the heart tissue slides and Dr. Guinn's opinions. Dr. Mann presently held the position of professor of pathology at Harvard Medical School and Massachusetts General Hospital . . . checkmate?

We set out to prove that the plaintiff's theory on the cause of Philip Long's heart attack was a Humpty Dumpty pile of assumptions. Our job was to take apart, brick by brick, the wall of assumptions supporting the expert's opinions. Show the jury that the opposing experts' assumptions were leaps of faith where medical facts were absent. Show the jury where the experts hurdled the gaps of logic between medical facts, and show the jury published medical research contradicting the experts' assumptions and opinions. It sounds easy, but it's not. And, of course, we had to be mindful of our own assumptions.

Someone once said, "It ain't what you don't know that gets you into trouble. It's what you know for sure that just ain't so." If you watch enough TV law dramas, you'll hear a senior lawyer knowingly tell a junior lawyer, "It's not what you know, it's what you can prove." That's true, but here is an additional caveat: Winning requires more than what I can prove; it's what a jury believes. At times, I have failed miserably at getting a jury to recognize that a highly qualified physician expert is spouting weak opinions. Yes, I have failed repeatedly in disproving the absolute certitude of experts on the witness stand. I don't eat breakfast or lunch when I'm in trial, but on the days I must cross-examine an expert testifying for their 50th time, the thought of food is as distant as the planet Venus.

After opening statements on the second day of trial, Dr. Janes, the plaintiff's handpicked coroner, strode to the witness stand. He raised his right hand and swore to tell the truth. Then, exuding confidence, he turned to the jury and explained that Philip Long died from severe atherosclerotic plaque buildup that caused a sudden cardiac death.

"In other words," he said, looking directly at the jury, "he literally dropped dead."

Dr. Janes skirted the lack of thrombus in the LAD by another convenient assumption, that a coronary spasm had blocked blood flow, a known complication of severe narrowing of coronary arteries from plaque buildup. Was there proof of an arterial spasm? No. But that was the assumption made to get around the absence of a thrombus. A constricted artery due to a spasm blocking blood flow made sense to a nonmedical person.

Mr. March had made the unusual move to hire two experts that contradicted each other. On cross-examination, I asked Dr. Janes if he agreed with the opinion of the newly hired plaintiff's cardiac pathologist, Dr. Guinn, that the autopsy he'd supervised was done incorrectly. Dr. Janes and Dr. Guinn were on the same side, yet they were presenting different *assumptions* on the cause of death: Dr. Janes said it was an arterial spasm; Dr. Guinn said it was clot from a plaque rupture. Dr. Janes would either have to agree he was wrong, or disagree with Dr. Guinn.

I asked Dr. Janes if he agreed with Dr. Guinn. He seemed unprepared for this question. He slouched on the witness stand for a moment, and then replied, "That's what he says."

Contradictory opinions between two experts on the same side of a case hang in the air like the stench of roadkill. This is no different than watching nightly political television programs, listening to experts disagree about decisions to employ economic sanctions, grant subsidies, or extend medical benefits. Disagreements between educated people create confusion. Confusion and loss of credibility are the enemies of persuasion. Did Dr. Janes make the wrong assumption about a narrowed coronary artery? If the jury dismissed the coroner's conclusion that an 80 percent blockage killed Mr. Long, then why did Mr. Long die? We believed the confusion in the plaintiff's case opened the door to *our version of the truth.*

Classic instruction on cross-examination techniques stresses *never ask a question you don't know the answer to*. For experienced trial lawyers, though, knowing the answer to a question before you ask a witness is not enough. Anticipating whether a medical expert will give an intellectually honest answer that can expose a faulty opinion takes a combination of experience, skill, and luck. And even then, expect the witness to be evasive. As lawyer Facher, the crusty defense lawyer described in the movie *A Civil Action*, might say, the truth may sink to the bottom of the bottomless pit.

The plaintiff's primary expert, Dr. Guinn, was a bespectacled gentleman with white hair and a starched white shirt under a dark suit, carrying his halo of Harvard credentials nonchalantly to the witness stand. On paper, I hadn't found a weakness.

On direct examination, Dr. Guinn made the case for a simple intervention that would have saved Mr. Long's life: Plavix, a blood thinner that prevents clotting. In Dr. Guinn's opinion, contrary to the coroner Dr. Janes, a clot had formed in the coronary artery. The sections of the coronary artery were sliced too thick, so the resident missed it. He argued there had to be a clot in the coronary artery because Mr. Long's heart stopped beating so quickly. Dr. Guinn assured the jury that Plavix or any other blood-thinning medication would have saved Mr. Long, even if a stent had not been placed to maintain an open passage in the coronary artery.

The plaintiff's lawyer was taking a great risk, presenting two pathologists with different theories on the cause of death. One said, "No plaque rupture, but spasm blocked the artery." The other said, "A clot blocked the artery and it was missed by the resident." We were in a giant chess match, trying to put the plaintiff's theories in check.

Dr. Guinn's authoritative pronouncements seemed bulletproof. Fortunately for us, he rarely strayed from a life of stone-cold bodies and squinting into a microscope.

As I got up to cross-examine Dr. Guinn, Amit nearly yanked my arm out of its socket. He whispered, "Ask him about medical literature. He's lying." Amit, like most doctors dragged into the courtroom, rage at loose assumptions.

I hesitated. Asking questions about medical literature I hadn't read was a setup for the classic harpoon in the chest. Using published medical research to impeach a witness is effective. What lawyers must avoid is taking quotes from one page of the article and then watching the opposing lawyer find a statement in the next page of same medical article supporting their theory in the case. But I trusted Dr. Rafi, so I took a chance.

"You don't treat patients, do you?" I asked nonchalantly.

"No, I don't," Dr. Guinn answered, smiling.

"Can you tell me how many times you've prescribed Plavix for a patient?"

"Never."

"So, in terms of incidence of the reduction of heart attacks in patients on Plavix, you would have no idea?"

"Ah . . . just from the literature," he admitted. "Personally, no."

Nervously, I asked Dr. Guinn if he knew the percentage of patients at risk for a heart attack taking Plavix that avoided having one. Amit held up two fingers to the jury. Fortunately, the plaintiff's counsel didn't see Amit's improper momentary lapse of my instructions: "Do not react to witness testimony."

"Offhand, I don't know what the actual percentages are," Dr. Guinn said apathetically. A surprisingly honest answer.

"In all fairness," I said, "it's not in your bailiwick to express an opinion on life-and-death matters when it comes to the use of Plavix."

"Not today, no," answered Dr. Guinn.

In today's world, experts abound in every discipline imaginable, from politics to beekeeping. Many won't admit they are outside their knowledge base, but surprisingly, that day, I got lucky.

When the trial continued the following week, our experts quoted statistics backed up by published research that Plavix reduced myocardial infarctions by only 2 percent. Was Dr. Guinn a liar? No, but he generalized and overstated the benefits of blood thinners. Baseless assumptions are not the same as lying, and lawyers know better than to call anyone a liar in the courtroom. Jurors recoil at harsh treatment of witnesses. They want to see passionate lawyers, but not nasty bullies.

Oh yeah, I was very proud of my cross of Dr. Guinn. But I knew I had been lucky. An expert more attuned to advocacy would have said, "Counsel, I have spent my life in medicine, and I can tell you that Plavix would have made a difference," and without the medical article at my fingertips, I'd have been harpooned again.

Amit Rafi's life *was* medicine. He nailed his testimony, giving the unmistakable image of a tireless doctor at the bedside, rushing into the cath lab to save lives. Amit scoffed at the assumption that Phil Long had suffered a coronary spasm due to plaque accumulation in his coronary artery. If that was the case, when the ambulance team administered nitroglycerin, a drug used to open constricted arteries, Phil's chest pain should have abated. It didn't. At the appropriate moment in his testimony, Amit pointed to his three-page consult note and told the jury that if he wrote down a recommendation for a test, any test, he made sure he told his patient.

Years before Amit Rafi's trial, I had read, "I'm OK, You're Biased," an op-ed piece in the *New York Times* by Harvard psychology professor Daniel Gilbert.[2] He wrote about "uncritically accepting evidence when it pleases us and insisting on more when it doesn't." We tip the scales of personal judgment toward those we favor. Professor Gilbert had referenced research showing that when we judge a person's abilities, we are inclined to ignore damning evidence about a person we like and continue to search for information "that might allow [us] to say something nice about him." This cognitive bias creates a "halo effect." In the courtroom, it causes jurors to find in favor of doctors who come across as conscientious and caring. Jurors overlook a likable doctor's errors more than those of a doctor they don't like. My client was a caring, confident, and professional doctor. But was that enough to topple the plaintiff's tower of assumptions?

Jury deliberations lasted a short two hours, usually a sign of a defense verdict. The jury found in favor of Dr. Rafi—no negligence. The foreman told us immediately after the verdict that the jury had believed Dr. Rafi

2. Daniel Gilbert, *I'm OK, You're Biased*, N.Y. Times, April 16, 2006, https://www.nytimes.com/2006/04/16/opinion/im-ok-youre-biased.html.

had told Mr. Long he should get a stress test, and that Mr. Long didn't tell his wife because he didn't want her to worry.

In the trial involving Amit Rafi, the plaintiff's lawyers relied on more assumptions than I had ever faced in the courtroom. There was the assumption that Amit never told the plaintiff he needed a stress test; Dr. Janes assumed the autopsy was done correctly; Dr. Guinn assumed a clot somewhere in the LAD killed the patient; Dr. Guinn assumed Plavix would have saved the day. However, the assumption that caused my burning gastric discomfort was the plaintiff's claim that Dr. Rafi didn't tell Mr. Long he needed a stress test. This discussion wasn't documented.

We had spent at least $100,000 developing our theory of causation in the hope that the jury would decide that stenting and Plavix would not have saved Mr. Long's life. We were concerned the jury wouldn't believe that Amit spoke with Mr. Long about a stress test, though we knew from the deposition of a witness we couldn't use that Phil hid his diabetic problems from his wife. Yet, we didn't win the case because of the money spent trying to persuade the jury on an alternative theory of why Phil Long died. Juries decide cases on gut instinct, often ignoring medical testimony, and I'm not heard complaining about jury assumptions that favor me and my clients. If there is one lesson I hope my readers take away from this book, it's that trial lawyers must be mindful of a jury's gut reaction to the plaintiff's themes of standard of care and causation. The jury liked Amit and believed Amit was a conscientious doctor. The jury believed Amit told Mr. Long he needed a stress test; thus the jury decided that Mr. Long was responsible for his own death.

26 Human Nature: No Guarantee of a Fair Trial

Lesson 26: People assume that the 7th Amendment's guarantee of the right to a jury trial equates to the expectation of a fair trial—don't count on it.

It's been said that jury trials are the "cutting edge of democracy." Theoretically, this statement is true. Theoretically, impartial individuals are chosen to sit on juries, historically serving as a hedge against overreaching state and federal prosecutors. Theoretically, juries weigh the testimony from both sides and make a fair decision based on the facts and sound logic.

According to James Podgers, a former editor of the *American Bar Association Journal*, "Jury trials provide insight into the human condition."

Therein lies the inherent flaw in our justice system. As I have mentioned, jurors decide cases based on personal experience, human emotion, and wonderment. Personal experience causes people to hear what they want to hear and see what they want to see. Facts, logic, and medical science won't persuade individuals blinded by their personal values. One common assumption held by people with no medical background is the belief that complications always happen to someone else, and if a complication happens to them, it's because someone else is at fault.

I always laugh to myself when I hear lawyers in medical malpractice cases tell juries that a "trial is a search for the truth." Doctors work in a world of uncertainty and are trained to embrace uncertainty. Patients as well as jurors look for and demand certitude where there is none. There is so much uncertainty in medicine that the best any lawyer can do is attempt to persuade a jury to accept their version of the medical truth.

Maybe it's always been true that people are swayed by anecdotes, narratives, and emotion; not so much by information as by the emotional content of a "really compelling story." Trial lawyers can present numerous statistics and facts, but it may not make any difference. I can't recall where I read this, but to me it best describes the beating heart of the courtroom.

Brian Manning's case still stings to this day. Brian wasn't too concerned about the blood-striped stools he flushed in the mornings. He'd had a bout of hemorrhoids five years ago and figured they were back. Robert, the physician's assistant who usually treated Brian, suspected hemorrhoids, too. When Robert examined Brian, he found no signs of bleeding. Because of Brian's age, no family history of cancer, and no episodes of wiping bright-red blood, Robert skipped performing the ever-joyful digital rectal examination on Brian. Instead, he prescribed hydrocortisone for hemorrhoidal itching and wrote in Brian's chart, "If he *continues* to have problems, he may warrant a referral for scoping." Seven weeks later, Brian called the doctor's office asking for more anti-itch cream. He didn't make an appointment to see the doctor, and Robert did not ask Brian to come into the office.

Six months later, Brian was diagnosed with terminal rectal cancer. An MRI showed that the cancer had spread to his liver and distant lymph nodes. Oncologists at the Toledo Clinic confirmed Stage IV cancer. The Clinic started him on "first-line treatment," the best combination of chemotherapy drugs based on his age, health, and biology of the cancer. Sadly, the chemo failed to halt the growing tumors in his liver and lymph nodes. Brian died less than two years after seeing blood in his stool, leaving behind a wife and three young daughters. He was 37.

Brian's death angered his wife. She believed the physician's assistant should have ordered more tests and diagnosed her husband's cancer eight months sooner. She sued Robert and his supervisor, Dr. Bradley, and Buckeye Health Services, a company that provided primary care doctors in Ohio and Michigan. Her lawyers would argue to the jury that Brian's symptoms warranted a colonoscopy either at the first visit or after the phone call for more medication, and the test would have discovered the tumor in the rectum. In a heart-rending moment, Mrs. Manning would cry out in the courtroom, "Brian was never given a fighting chance."

Procedurally, plaintiffs usually file lawsuits in the county where the alleged negligence occurred. But plaintiffs have the right to sue defendants in the county where they reside or have another place of business. Jurors in smaller communities are less likely to find the local town doctor negligent, and rural juries typically don't award large money verdicts. "Forum shopping" is a common tactical move by plaintiff's lawyers to find jurors more inclined to award big-money damages.

Buckeye Health Services had offices in Toledo. So, Mrs. Manning's lawyers filed the malpractice case in Toledo, 60 miles away from the small town where Dr. Bradley and Robert practiced.

Mrs. Manning's lawyers tapped into the cottage industry of experts-for-hire willing to second-guess the diagnosis of hemorrhoids. My experts, well-credentialed and with years of experience on the witness stand, believed that the plaintiff could not prove causation—that early treatment would not have saved Brian's life. Some cancers are a death notice whether discovered early or late.

One of the more recent discoveries in cancer research reveals that a certain percentage of cancers are hard-wired to rapidly metastasize very early in the formation of the tumor. And cancer research has uncovered that it's not just the size of the tumor, but the biology of the specific type of cancer, that causes some cancers to spread more quickly.

One of our experts, a colorectal surgeon and former examiner for the American Board of Colon and Rectal Surgery who I had used before, would explain that the molecular makeup of Brian's tumors preordained his rapid spread of cancer. And a sad reality of many types of cancers, like rectal tumors, was their failure to respond to therapy. Early diagnosis in many aggressive tumors may do very little to prolong life.

Our search of medical literature told us this much: rectal tumors grow slowly and are typically advanced by the time they become symptomatic. This is why doctors recommend screening colonoscopies at ages 45 and 50. In young patients, however, colon and rectal cancer may be aggressive and terminal by the time any signs of a tumor appear. But the risk of rectal cancer in men under 45, with no family history of colon or rectal cancer, is extremely low—this was the reason Robert didn't feel it was necessary to screen for rectal cancer for his 35-year-old patient.

Rectal malignancy in a 35-year-old meant only one thing to me: By the time Brian walked into Dr. Bradley's office, neither surgery nor chemotherapy would have altered his destiny. I expected we would easily win this case.

On the morning of jury selection, I eyeballed 30 or so potential jurors as they took their seats in the courtroom. As a defense attorney, I'm mindful of jurors inclined to hand the plaintiff's lawyers the keys to Fort Knox. The first potential juror was a guy wearing a grunge T-shirt and dyed his hair, who wouldn't have looked out of place at an Alice in Chains concert. I look for telltale signs of left-leaning believers: a beard, a ponytail, union workers, social workers, the unemployed, the innocence of youth, and anyone inclined to believe the government owes them something.

I confess that race is a factor in the choice of jurors. I believe all attorneys keep ethnicity, race, and gender in mind. This concern has more to do with respecting the human condition than personal prejudice, but it's a bias just the same. It's a lot to ask a person who has suffered lifelong institutional discrimination in jobs, equal pay, equal opportunities, access to healthcare, police profiling, slurs, and slights to set personal experience aside and empathize with the police, insurance companies, hospitals, and doctors. We ask all jurors to forget their past and swear under oath that each side starts out on an equal playing field. But unless you grew up in an ice cave at the North Pole, you know that the burning pain of human suffering is not so easily put on ice. Black or Brown college-educated jurors and jurors working in jobs that require more than just "showing up" are the exception to my bias. I'm sorry if this is offensive, but trial attorneys have an obligation to their clients. When I sued doctors, white dudes wearing navy sport coats and paisley ties working for corporate America were the first to go.

I usually announce, at the start of jury selection, that I'm not prying into anyone's personal life—which is exactly what I am doing. I say that our intent is to choose fair and impartial jurors to sit in judgment of this case. Of course, that's not true either. (If your lawyer tells *you* they aim to choose fair and impartial jurors, fire him or her immediately.) There is no such beast as a fair and impartial juror, no matter what a juror believes or promises in the courtroom. There are only those jurors who can or cannot be persuaded to accept my version of truth and reality.

For example, eight Black jurors and one Hispanic juror out of 12 selected to hear a murder case in Los Angeles with evidence of the police brutalizing Black citizens might be receptive to the argument that police planted damning evidence linking a defendant (a popular black athlete) to the murder of his ex-wife and her friend. A juror's education level, employment, and life experience shape jurors' perception of evidence.

Thomas Jefferson deposited enormous faith in the jury system, saying, "I consider trial by jury as the only anchor ever yet imagined by man, by which a government can be held to the principles of its constitution." Mr. Jefferson surely presumed that a group of white male landowners representing the "conscience of the community" would come together and make a moral and true decision based on the facts. Men who spent years on death row, their convictions based on racial bias and exonerated decades later by DNA analysis, rightfully come to a different conclusion.

I consider more telling the quote delivered by Will Durant, the great historian who, in collaboration with his wife Ariel Durant, wrote the 11-volume Pulitzer Prize–winning *The Story of Civilization*. "Nature has never read the Declaration of Independence. It continues to make us unequal." If they were alive today and were questioned about the Seventh Amendment, I'm certain they would add their pessimism about human nature's ability to treat all people equally and deliver a fair trial.

Our evidence on Brian's misfortune went in as expected: a young man stricken with rectal cancer, a relentless and indestructible biological force. We presented evidence on cancer research that showed how the cell biology of tumors had shifted doctors' thinking about survival. Luck and genetics may be more important to survival than the best available chemotherapy. We presented evidence highlighting the date of Brian's telephone call for more rectal cream and *his* failure to follow up with the doctor. I delicately tried to seed the thought that Brian shared responsibility for his own delayed diagnosis.

We hired cancer experts with luminous credentials compared to the lesser-qualified plaintiff's experts. One of our themes emphasized the aggressive growth of rectal cancer in young patients. Our cancer expert pointed out that at the time Brian saw Robert, his cancer was in its last stage. Diagnosis at that time would not have prevented his untimely death.

Brian's cancer had only partially responded to chemotherapy. Tumors in his lymph nodes continued to grow. Our expert told the jury that if the metastatic cancer cells fought off chemotherapy in the cancer's late stages, chemotherapy in the early stage most likely would have been ineffective. Treatment eight months earlier probably would not have changed the outcome.

There were no surprises in the plaintiff's experts' testimony. But it wasn't the experts that caused me to grit my teeth. In cancer cases, the plaintiff may die before the trial date. Plaintiff's lawyers hire professional videographers to film deathbed testimony and display the carnage of metastatic cancer. Before trial, I had read the transcript of the video but hadn't watched the playback. The video opened with an image of Brian. He was emaciated; his face gaunt, his skin yellow from liver failure, eyeballs sucked deep into their sockets. Unable to lift his head from the pillow, he barely spoke above a whisper, forcing every breath.

Plaintiff's counsel asked him to set the record straight.

In a heart-rending, raspy whisper, he said he first realized Robert didn't give him a proper rectal exam after he was examined and diagnosed at the Toledo Clinic. Robert only did a visual examination, Brian said. One of the plaintiff's experts had argued that the tumor was big enough and close enough to have been felt with a digital exam, an assumption that made sense, but unlikely. As the video of a dying young man decimated by cancer and teetering on the precipice of darkness played to the jury, I felt the bottom of the courtroom give way. I could hear the jurors' hearts break.

It got worse.

Brian said, "My hope is that [my wife] and my daughters continue on and live a life that is full of happiness and peace and know that I'm with them, whether I'm here or not. I want them to know . . . that God is with them . . . I'm still with them; that I love them." Jumbled in this heartfelt plea to the jury, Brian spoke more of his wife. "We had an opportunity to do some nice things together in life and—but I know that stuff is dwindling down. It's hurtful to, you know, miss out on that time with your family, very hurtful."

As painful as it was to watch a dying man long for the intimacy of his family, I still held on to the belief that the jury would fault Brian for his lapse in personal responsibility. A senior trial lawyer from our office questioned Brian in a nonthreatening, conversational style about his failure to follow up with his doctor as instructed.

Toward the end of the video, Brian struggled to roll his head to one side. "Could I have a sip of water?" he whispered. I had my game face securely fastened. I kept asking myself *can this get any worse?*, and it did. It's never a good thing when the wife sobs in the courtroom. Worse yet, when jurors tear up, too.

The final argument went well, I thought. I showed the jury the transcript of Brian's testimony. I didn't say, "Brian was negligent." That language would fall into the category of kicking a guy when he's down. But I pointed out that the delay in diagnosis began when Brian failed to make a follow-up appointment when his bleeding continued. The idea was to lead the jury to the conclusion that Brian was a noncompliant patient. The plaintiff's lawyer countered with Robert's superior knowledge and responsibility to advise his client of the importance to come into the office, since Brian's problem should have cleared up by then.

I presented medical research and current data showing that rectal cancer in 35-year-olds doesn't end well. Plaintiff's counsel rebutted our scientific arguments, telling the jury, "Don't let the defense lawyers get away with these excuses." He deftly refocused the jury to think about safety in medicine and what the jurors would want for themselves. "What would I do if this were me?"

We objected to this line of argument, because jurors will focus on themselves and decide to make the world a better place, instead of determining whether the doctor met the standard of care. Sickness and disease have never been fair, but in the current American culture of *social justice*, there must be someone to blame. Think about it: During the course of writing this manuscript, there have been catastrophic floods, fires decimating entire communities, mass shootings, and storms. Inevitably, a news organization, county officials, or a politician will point the finger at someone or some organization that could have or should have seen this coming or been better prepared and had failed in some way to provide timely warning of the danger and should be made to pay. Still, I had a good feeling when I sat down after my final argument. Usually, juries are unforgiving when the plaintiff doesn't follow the doctor's orders or recommendations. The patient gets the blame.

On the morning of the verdict, I was attending a deposition in another case. The senior lawyer who'd tried the case with me called moments after the verdict. I could tell by his tone it was bad.

How bad?

Over $5 million bad.

After the verdict, we hired a jury consultant to conduct juror interviews, asking what evidence the jury found helpful in reaching their decision. Discussing a case with jurors after a verdict is semi-enlightening. The real skinny comes during one-on-one conversations, outside the courtroom. Only one juror was willing to talk to the consultant.

Reading the older, educated female juror's comments was depressing. I believe I lost the jury after they watched the video in the plaintiff's case. The jury felt Brian's pain. How else could the jury ignore medical science, our highly credentialed experts, and the recent advances in cancer biology that unlocked the mystery of why some cancer patients succumb and others live a long time?

The college-educated juror said the defense didn't have strong arguments. "The defense kept saying he had Stage IV when he went into the doctor's office. *I don't believe it.* He was a healthy 35-year-old."

Our experts told the jury that a doctor would not have ordered a colonoscopy on a young man with a history of hemorrhoids on the first visit. The suspicion of cancer would be exceedingly low. Guidelines for colorectal screening at that time recommended screening at age 50.

The jury concluded otherwise. The juror said, "You can't say he had Stage IV cancer on the first visit, and then argue he was a healthy 35-year-old who wouldn't need a colonoscopy. Statistics are just statistics. . . ."

The fine line distinction between age, slow-growing cancer, and indications for testing was lost on the jury. The plaintiff's attorney argued Brian was in the early stage of cancer. But there was no way to definitively prove Brian's stage of cancer eight months before his diagnosis. The jury accepted the plaintiff's version of the truth that the cancer went from stage 1 to terminal in 8 months.

"We never discussed the experts' [testimony], they had *no data,*" the juror reported to the jury consultant. *Huh?* I have to say that there is an element of futility in trial work. A response like this reinforces my belief that scientific explanations are not enough in the courtroom.

A recipe for large verdicts defying scientific evidence is nothing new: a sympathetic young widow with three darling daughters, her husband dying on camera, and stoic defendant doctors who appeared anything but warm and fuzzy on the witness stand. Emotional jurors pay little attention to facts. I kept telling the jury that a slow-growing cancer doesn't suddenly go from Stage I to Stage IV in less than eight months. I have had to try many cases that engender strong emotional pull. Usually jurors fight off the undertow of heartfelt emotions and find for the doctor. The clincher here, though, was that the plaintiffs told a more emotionally compelling story.

According to the juror our consultant interviewed, all of the experts were completely ignored. Why do intelligent people who know absolutely nothing about molecular biology, know absolutely nothing about the pathways of metastatic disease, and the difference between remission and a cure, refuse to embrace scientific evidence? To me the answer is . . . we were unlucky with the jury pool, and we did not have an emotional human-interest story to tell. Yet, I always think back about what I could have done better. We didn't call one of our expert witnesses at the end of our evidence. We thought the jury was on our side. After reading the jury consultant's report, I don't think calling an additional expert would have changed the outcome.

I have been using validated statistical medical evidence in the courtroom for decades. It's persuasive most of the time, but when it's not, I think about why. Since the 1950s, research on cognitive failure has confirmed that we humans have a predilection to parse new data to support preexisting beliefs and reject arguments or information that doesn't. "It's more than 'confirmation bias,'" wrote Lisa Rosenbaum, MD, Assistant Professor of Medicine at Brigham and Women's Hospital, a Harvard teaching hospital. In an article published in the *New England Journal of Medicine*,[1] she said what's at work here is a phenomenon called "biased assimilation." "First," Dr. Rosenbaum says, "we need to stop assuming that disbelief necessarily reflects a knowledge deficit and thus can be remedied by facts." What's scary is more education, more facts, and more science only "backfires."

Jury consultants almost unanimously tell trial lawyers that a well-told story is more persuasive than laying out the facts. Juries don't easily digest scientific evidence derived from expert witnesses trying to explain the results of years of research in five-minute segments from the witness stand. Drury Sherrod, the author of *The Jury Crisis: What's Wrong with Jury Trials and How We Can Save Them*, writes that when juries don't understand, they "rely on 'stored scripts' from their own lives" to make sense of complicated facts. In short, a well-told story of cherry-picked information may be a better version of the truth.

The night after the $5 million verdict, I sat alone on my balcony, looking out at the Columbus skyline. I nursed my bourbon and thought about what I had done wrong. Why did I so badly misread this jury? Did I kick off the wrong jurors? Did I spend enough time warning the jury about hindsight? Would more statistics have made a difference? This case confirmed in my mind one very disturbing fact about the way we are. There are individuals, groups, and even communities where reason proves

1. Lisa Rosenbaum, MD, *Resisting the Suppression of Science*, 376 NEJM 17 (2017).

useless: criminal minds, religious zealots, and captains of businesses, big and small, with vested interest in profit, just to name a few. Thomas Jefferson believed "all men are created equal." We know he meant this in regard to treatment under the law. But we know better. Some people can be educated to search for knowledge and meaning beyond their personal beliefs and interests. Many cannot.

27 Legal Malpractice or a Money Grab?

Lesson 27: Sometimes settlement is a bitter pill, but know when to cut your losses.

One afternoon, the year before my partner Gayle Arnold died, he called me into his office. "Shut the door," he said. Before I could sit in the chair across from his large mahogany desk, Gayle handed me a copy of a lawsuit. As I read it, my heart started pounding. A former client, a chiropractor, was suing our law firm.

I searched for my name. *Please don't let me be the dumb shit that got us sued.* I wasn't. The acid level in my stomach subsided and the cold steel pliers that had locked around my sphincter slowly released their grip. The defendant named in the lawsuit was Jim Glass, a trial lawyer formerly employed by Arnold & Associates. I knew him as a hardworking, knowledgeable, train-on-its-track lawyer.

Gayle asked me to pull the old medical records and search the electronic file. He wanted to know if this was a "money grab," or if we had something to worry about. He wanted an answer before he called our malpractice insurance carrier, a moment of dread for any lawyer.

Alex Banks, a 30-year-old entry-level stockbroker, had suffered from head and neck pain. His chiropractor, Dr. Leonard (our former client), typically performed spinal manipulations in his office. On the morning of Alex's manipulation, he began to have breathing problems.

Alex had stopped breathing after Dr. Leonard had manipulated his neck and back. Alex was left unattended for 15 minutes. Once notified, Dr. Leonard started desperately pushing on Alex's chest while his assistant squeezed a ventilation bag, forcing air into Alex's lungs. The emergency squad arrived 15 minutes later. An injection of powerful, heart-stimulating drugs kickstarted Alex's heart, but his brain was dead.

Dr. Leonard's manipulation was over agressive and caused diaphragmatic paralysis and Alex stopped breathing. Left unattended he suffered severe brain damage.

Alex's wife, Rhonda, sued Dr. Leonard for malpractice.

The defense of any doctor begins with finding a similar specialist to review the medical records. Jim Glass had dutifully knocked on the doors of potential experts: chiropractors, orthopeadic doctors, and family osteopathic physicians. The answer was always the same: the standard of care required continuous monitoring of a patient who has breathing problems postmanipulation and should be evaluated and monitored

Unable to find any experts to defend Dr. Leonard, Jim ponied up $1 million—all the insurance money Dr. Leonard had—to settle the lawsuit. Rhonda's lawyer demanded assurances that Dr. Leonard didn't have a huge pot of money hidden away in savings. The settlement was a good deal for Dr. Leonard: A jury could return a verdict of more than $10 million for a plaintiff in a vegetative state. Rhonda would have owned Dr. Leonard for life.

Rhonda signed a release of all claims against Dr. Leonard for $1 million. The plaintiff's lawyer received a nice fee without going to trial. Dr. Leonard closed the book on this stressful chapter in his life. Jim had done the best he could, given the facts—so he thought.

For the next five years, Alex existed in a vegetative state. Then one morning his father pulled the plug. Mr. Banks, now the administrator of Alex's estate, immediately filed a wrongful death claim on behalf of himself and other family members for the loss of love, society, and friendship with Alex. The wrongful death claim was legitimate, despite Alex's father voluntarily terminating his son's life. Because Alex's wife had signed the release, she couldn't join in the lawsuit for wrongful death. Rhonda's lawsuit was for Alex's pain and suffering and Rhonda's loss of love and affection—a different claim than the wrongful death claim brought by the heirs. The potential verdict was nothing to lose sleep over, unless you were Dr. Leonard, with no insurance money left to pay the family.

"This is another fine mess you got me into," I said to Gayle, my stock response to complicated cases. "This case is nothing but a money grab. Alex's wife settled, his father pulled the plug, now the rest of his family sues Dr. Leonard for causing Alex's death. And get this: Our grateful chiropractor is out of insurance, so he sues our law firm for legal malpractice so that the good doctor can get the money from us to pay off Alex's family."

"What did Jim do wrong?" Gayle asked.

"Dr. Leonard," I said, "claims that Jim *should* have made the family and next of kin sign the same release Rhonda signed to waive their rights to bring a wrongful death claim, even though Alex was still alive."

"Should he have?" Gayle asked.

"Hell, no. Two years before Jim settled Dr. Leonard's case, the Ohio Supreme Court struck down the statutory law allowing family members to release their wrongful death claims while their loved one was still alive. At the time Jim settled the case for Dr. Leonard, Alex was alive and other than Alex's wife, other family members couldn't lawfully release their future wrongful death claims."

Gayle wanted to know how much the family wanted.

"Millions," I told him.

"Really?"

"Yeah," I nodded. "Really."

Rarely do legal malpractice cases go to trial. Dear reader, I hope you are not shocked to hear that lawyers are widely perceived as sleazy, greedy, and manipulative. And it's not the money that wrecks the lawyer's sleep cycle; it's the fragile reputations of lawyers who strive to rise above the bucket of scum where many people believe they belong who are stained in the aftermath of a malpractice lawsuit, win or lose. Decades of hard-earned respectability and prominence in the legal community can be undone by a jury in two hours. It's different for doctors. If they are sued, the medical community is sympathetic. But the brotherhood of lawyers is heard to snicker, "Did you hear? Glass got sued. He must have screwed up somewhere."

Legal malpractice insurance companies typically allow the accused attorneys to choose from a preapproved list of insurance defense attorneys who have agreed to a negotiated billing rate. I had sued several large law firms when I did plaintiff's work. I was the only one on our malpractice carrier's preapproved list with combined experience in legal and medical malpractice as both a plaintiff and defense lawyer. Gayle and I decided I was the best lawyer to defend Jim and the firm. We agreed that, if necessary, we would fight this all the way to the Ohio Supreme Court.

Doctors and lawyers sued for malpractice see themselves as victims of liars and greed. Trial lawyers must maintain an emotional distance from their clients; not easily done when you're one and the same.

The claims supervisor from our insurance company didn't say it, but I knew what she was thinking: "A lawyer who represents himself has a fool for a client."

Despite her reservations, I got the assignment.

Know your judge. That's dogma in the world of trial lawyers. Know the background of the lawyer sitting in judgment of you and your case; know their politics, their judicial temperament, their legal experience, and their willingness to respect the rules of evidence and procedure. Are they fair? Are they lazy? Do they control their courtroom or do the lawyers flail at each other like teenagers? Are their rulings timely or does it take the judge nine months to decide a motion? Will they follow the law or do they decide issues based on political affiliations? Trial judges, unlike the U.S. Supreme Court and state supreme courts, don't decide policy issues. And not to be ignored is the judge's staff. Are they helpful? Or have they forgotten they are "public servants" and act like they are doing a favor when a lawyer makes a request?

I've learned to deal with the biases and prejudices of jurors, combative opponents, and disingenuous witnesses. I have yet to find a way to overcome a trial judge who favors my opponent or dislikes my case or my client. Judges are empowered with sweeping discretion to admit or exclude evidence and witnesses' testimony—meaning they have the power to destroy your case.

The position of trial judge is not an entry-level job, but it pays like one. My more sarcastic brethren like to say that lawyers who can't make it in private practice run for judge. I once handed an Ohio Supreme Court judge running for reelection my personal check for $1,000. Thinking he was paying me a compliment, he surprisingly said the same thing.

It's rare—extremely rare—that a moderately successful lawyer earning $200,000 (or more) per year will run for the elected office of state court trial judge. In Ohio, the current starting judicial salary is approximately $125,000. The prestige of a federal judgeship is one of the few exceptions. Yet, I've seen federal judges leave for better financial opportunities. Unless a trial lawyer has a health issue or prefers regular hours, I don't see financially successful lawyers taking a pay cut to run for judicial office in state court. Thus, young and inexperienced lawyers and lawyers who failed to develop a successful practice line up for the ballot box in Ohio. As one senior judge lamented at a recent judicial candidate's fundraiser, "My socks are older than her." In Ohio, six years after a lawyer is licensed, they're qualified to run for judicial office.

Judge Gordon, assigned to our case, ran for municipal court 30 years ago in a rural town 70 miles south of Columbus; the full-time position paid $31,000. Hard-charging young lawyers at established firms were making twice that amount. He crept into the ballot box seven years out of law school. Lawyer Gordon was part of this trend of judicial candidates running for office, bereft of any distinguished credentials and experience, intent on working their way up the judicial ladder.

In the 1990s, Judge Gordon, by the good graces of politics, landed a job as elections counsel for the state of Ohio. By the late 1990s, he moved on to the office that researched and compiled crime statistics. What expertise did this job provide to prepare a lawyer for higher judicial office? None, of course.

Eventually, the Ohio governor appointed Gordon to the Franklin County Common Pleas Court to fill a vacancy. Judge Gordon lost reelection the following year. Ohio governors have a habit of reappointing judges voted out of office to fill judicial vacancies. Of course, the governor appointed Gordon to fill a judicial vacancy in Columbus. This time he was reelected.

By luck of the draw, the Franklin County Assignment Commissioner assigned Judge Gordon to our legal malpractice case. By reputation, he was not a bad judge in criminal matters where the legal issues were routine and simplistic, but he had mixed reviews in civil cases—*indecisive* was the word on the street.

Most legal malpractice cases can be resolved by the judge's decisions in the motion stage of the case. A judge's decision may eviscerate the plaintiff's case, leading to an outright dismissal or a nuisance settlement. On the other hand, the judge can make a ruling that forces the defendant to fork over a hefty chunk of money.

Judge Gordon seemed perplexed during our first status conference—understandable given the three-headed monster on his docket. Alex's family sued Dr. Leonard. Dr. Leonard sued Arnold & Associates (now Arnold, Todaro, Welch & Foliano).

Alex Banks's father made clear he was not after money. He wanted vengeance. We discovered that he'd planned to sue Dr. Leonard before disconnecting his son from life support. At his deposition, I asked Mr. Banks about the timing of the lawsuit. He answered, in high dudgeon, "I want to wreck his life like he wrecked my son."

At our first status conference in Judge Gordon's chambers, discussions about the liability of the defendants and the rights of the family to file a lawsuit circled the conference table like a dog chasing its tail. Judge Gordon listened to the circuitous arguments among the lawyers, obviously struggling with the novel legal issues and tangled principles of law arising out of a legal malpractice case.

In July of 2007, Gayle headed to his lake house in Michigan to spend two weeks with his family. He walked into my office with his briefcase loaded with files, parked himself in the chair across from my desk and said, "Bring me up to speed on the Leonard case."

I assured him the law was on our side. "We've got a silver bullet," I said. "The defense of *judgmental immunity* should get the case dismissed. They can't second-guess a lawyer for legal decision when the law controlling the decision is in a state of flux."

Gayle looked discouraged. "What's your guess that Gordon will get it?"

"I'm optimistic," I said. I pointed out that Gordon's staff attorney, whom the judge depended on to spoon-feed him the law, was academically inclined. I was sure he would understand the law and its application to the facts of this case.

Gayle, a trial lawyer with decades of experience, seemed worried. "The only party with money in this fiasco is us. We're the only one with insurance."

Then he was off to his summer home in the "state up north." I would never see him alive again. Gayle died of a heart attack six days later. He was 57.

At the next status conference with Judge Gordon, I raised the defense of *judgmental immunity*, a defense completely exonerating Jim from liability. Judge Gordon was unfamiliar with the legal theory protecting lawyers from lawsuits when the appeals courts are undecided on the application of a principle of law governing a dispute.

"It's unique to legal malpractice cases," I explained to the judge. "When a legal principle governing the outcome of a dispute based on similar facts is unsettled because the lower court's opinions contradict one another (or as in this case, where there is no law at all), it's not fair to base a lawsuit on one appellate decision that favors your side of the case, when other appellate cases come to the opposite conclusion."[1] Until the Ohio Supreme Court decides the issue, that principle of law is in a state of flux.

I reminded the judge that normally a wrongful death lawsuit has two claims. The survivorship action, that involved Alex's medical expenses and pain and suffering, and the spouse's loss of love and society up to the time Alex died. The wrongful death claim of loss of future income and loss of society by spouse or next of kin is a viable claim only after death. However, legislation allowing a wrongful death claim to be settled before the plaintiff dies was not on the books when Alex's wife settled his pain and suffering claim. I explained to Judge Gordon the chronology:

- 1994: The Ohio Supreme Court ruled that a wrongful death claim action can't be settled until the injured plaintiff dies.
- 1996: In response to the high court's decision, the Ohio state legislature—at the urging of the insurance industry—passed a law authorizing settlement of wrongful death claims *before* the severely damaged plaintiff died. The statute made it legal for insurance companies to wrap up all future claims of potential heirs, even if the injured plaintiff was still alive. At the time of settlement, the insurance lawyer could have everyone with a potential claim sign a release.
- 1999: The Ohio Supreme Court ruled the 1996 statute unconstitutional.
- 2001: Jim settled the malpractice case against Dr. Leonard. Obviously, there was no law in effect validating the next of kin settling future wrongful death claims or next of kin releasing their future wrongful death claims.

I explained that Rhonda's release did not include signatures for Alex's dad, mom, sisters, or grandparents, because in 2001 there was no law validating the releases signed by potential heirs. Even if Alex's family members signed a release or waiver of all claims, they would be invalid

1. For example, an appellate court in Cleveland ruled that smoking pot in your home was legal, and an appellate court in Cincinnati ruled that it was illegal. Your client in Columbus wants to hold a pot party in his home, but Columbus hasn't yet ruled on this issue. Your advice to your client approving a pot party should not be subject to attack on the basis of the ruling from the appellate court in Cincinnati or the appellate court in Columbus ruling, two years after the pot party, that pot parties are against the law.

and the heirs could still sue Dr. Leonard for the wrongful death of Alex after he died.

I told Judge Gordon that there couldn't be a clearer situation of unsettled law. The doctrine of *judgmental immunity* shields lawyers in Jim's situation from malpractice for failing to perform a legal act which is an exercise in futility.

Dr. Leonard's lawyer disagreed, arguing that two adult people can contract to do anything. Jim should have contacted all the family members and negotiated small sums in exchange for their signature on the release signed by Rhonda.

"It's ridiculous," I argued, "to say that a lawyer was negligent for failing to do something he can't legally do." I told the judge that our experts would testify that probate court controls wrongful death settlements, and under probate law, only the executor (the authorized party by statute) of Alex's estate could legally waive future claims of potential heirs. But Alex was not dead, there was no estate set up, and his wife was not appointed as an executor or executrix of Alex's estate; thus the potential heirs could not legally release future claims even if they signed a release.

Dr. Leonard, now retired, wanted our firm to ante up the money the family wanted so he could settle with the family. Dr. Leonard's lawyer claimed his client could scrape together no more than five figures. Gayle was right. The only defendant with a deep pocket, lined by insurance money to pay off the family, was us.

In the next election cycle, a glimmer of hope appeared: Judge Gordon was up for reelection. As in many states, Ohio selects judges by popular vote. Judicial candidates and sitting judges campaign for cash (I mean, reelection) like any other politician. They hold fundraisers, pester lawyers for money, and purchase TV time to pander the slogan "I'm tough on crime." Lawyers hate election season, especially the sitting judges who make personal calls for donations, and truly, judges hate the process just as much as lawyers do.

Only nonlawyers assume a judge's competence from prior judicial service. Moon landings are more common than letters to the editor written by practicing lawyers criticizing the competence or fairness of a sitting judge. "Grin and bear it" was a common refrain.

The fault in Ohio's system lies in the general public's ignorance of the qualifications of judicial candidates. The half-page of autobiographical information printed on campaign brochures, or, in recent years, found on the internet, says nothing about the quality of the candidate. And frankly, a lawyer six years out of law school has neither the experience nor the wisdom to handle the complexity of serious cases.

As for Judge Gordon, political backscratching vanquished any hope of a newly elected judge taking over our case. In Ohio, occasionally the political bosses of the local Democratic and Republican parties trade judgeships. An incumbent Republican judge runs unopposed and an incumbent Democratic judge the same year has no opposition. All too often, a judge runs unopposed because their name recognition from years on the bench makes it difficult to unseat them, despite their mediocre performance as a judge. The party bosses don't waste money on candidates who can't win. This time Judge Gordon ran unopposed. So did a Democratic candidate for judicial office that same year.

***

At the end of each status conference, Judge Gordon asked where we were on settlement. A lawsuit missing a grieving spouse and fatherless children lacked the emotional slap that transforms juries into cash registers spitting money. I believed the evidence that Alex's father essentially ended his son's life so that he could sue Dr. Leonard would alienate the jury. During the trial, Alex's father would smooth over his decision by explaining, "We knew he would never wake up and we couldn't stand to see him suffer anymore." However, Alex was brain dead. He was not suffering.

The money the family claimed Dr. Leonard owed them had to be resolved first. The family's demand for millions prevented any chance for settlement. The Banks family's lawyer was counting on us pressing our insurance company to pay an exorbitant sum on behalf of Dr. Leonard so Jim could avoid the embarrassment of trial. In fact, I went back and forth in my mind about what was best for Jim: settle or fight the money-grubbing bastards. (Every lawsuit seems like a money grab when you're defending yourself in a legal malpractice case.)

With negotiations at an impasse, Judge Gordon scheduled the family's case against Dr. Leonard for trial. Given that Dr. Leonard could not be defended on the standard of care, the sole issue for the jury was *how much*? The jury wouldn't hear about Rhonda's previous settlement of the survival claim or that Medicaid had paid Alex's actual medical expenses, not Alex's wife. Evidence of sympathy-charged testimony about Alex's vegetative state and pain and suffering *before* he died was not relevant. That evidence is relevant in the survival claim, not the wrongful death claim. Pain and suffering was the basis of the settlement with Rhonda. Now the only issue for the jury was the loss of love and affection, guidance, inheritance, and so on of Alex's family members.

Surprisingly, Judge Gordon allowed family members to testify about Alex's paralyzed condition, gnarled hands and feet, and the strain on the family before Alex died. Dr. Leonard's attorney jumped to his feet, vigorously objecting to this testimony. He reminded Judge Gordon that testimony about Alex's pain and suffering before death was inadmissible. Yet Judge Gordon overruled the objection and allowed the family to wrench tears of sympathy from the jury. However, at the end of the trial, Judge Gordon recognized his error. He instructed the jury they should not, after all, consider the family's suffering before death.

Trial lawyers know such an instruction is a useless admonition. You can't unring a bell; the human condition won't allow the mind to erase what it once heard. The kneejerk decision to overrule the defense counsel's objection had effectively doomed Dr. Leonard's chances of containing the verdict. The jury's verdict was twice the amount we expected.

After the verdict, Judge Gordon joked at one of our status conferences that the court of appeals would have their hands full with this case, a sign that he was unsure of how to rule on the issues. He again tried to settle Dr. Leonard's case against Jim and our law firm. The family wouldn't budge off their verdict close to a million dollars. And why should they? A jury had spoken. Now Dr. Leonard had to go after us to get money to pay off the verdict.

So the lawsuit wasn't about wrecking Dr. Leonard, was it? It was about money. The family's lawyer assumed we would avoid the stigma of negligence and press our insurance company to pay. But I had no intention of groveling. I was confident a jury would see that Jim had done all he could legally do to protect Dr. Leonard.

About a year before the trial date, I filed a motion to dismiss the lawsuit against Jim and our law firm based on the complete defense of "judgmental immunity." Dr. Leonard's lawyer disagreed. He found a recent, obscure unreported appellate decision out of Youngstown, Ohio. It held that family members could waive future wrongful death claims before the death of the plaintiff.

I attached to my motion a sworn statement signed by a retired probate judge from Cleveland, declaring, "The standard of care required of an attorney cannot be based on one unreported court of appeals decision and more importantly in a different appellate district in which the attorney was practicing law."

Eleven months later, Judge Gordon denied our motion to dismiss. In his decision, he stated, "the Supreme Court of Ohio has not expressly adopted the [judgmental immunity] rule, we decline to apply it in this instance."

It is not wrong for a judge to look to an appellate court for guidance. I didn't like the ruling because it was not controlling law in our appellate district. My assumption here is that the judge did not want to dismiss the case and his staff attorney found a reed-thin legal reason for denying my motion.

Four months later, we began selecting a jury.

Dr. Leonard's evidence unfolded in the courtroom as expected. After he finished his evidence, our experts marched to the witness stand. Their message was consistent and clear: As long as Alex was alive, the family couldn't legally release future wrongful death claims. The standard of care did not require a lawyer to obtain releases from family members.

Toward the end of a trial, judges will ask the lawyers to submit last-minute jury instructions. Jury instructions outline the issues for the jury, define legal terms, and guide the jurors' conduct during deliberations. Juries are always advised that they are the sole judge of the facts and believability of the witnesses, and are instructed on the principles of law that apply to the case. Jury instructions are predicated on well-settled law. Jury instructions emphasize that jurors must follow the law, regardless of whether they like the law or think the law should be different.

I arrived 15 minutes before our 8:30 a.m. meeting in Judge Gordon's chambers to discuss jury instructions. Standing outside the chambers, sipping my third cup of Oklahoma crude, I saw Judge Gordon walking down the hallway.

He smiled broadly as we greeted each other. "Jerry," he said, "I've decided, I'm ruling as a matter of law that potential heirs can waive future wrongful death claims." He planned to instruct the jury accordingly.

Back then, I was much better at holding my tongue. I wanted to scream, "What f_______ law are you talking about?"

I huddled with Jim and my co-counsel. Once the jury heard the judge—the man in the black robe—pronounce that the law allows the family to waive their future claims, we were screwed. The jury would punish Jim for not following the law. We couldn't argue that Judge

Gordon made a mistake. Any errors in the instructions of law to the jury must be appealed to a higher court.

In opening statement, I had stood center court, my demeanor infused with conviction, embroidering on the jury's mind that there was no law that allowed my client to secure a valid release. Now, jurors would think I had lied. The inevitable plaintiff's verdict would brand Jim for a lifetime as a negligent lawyer—a reputation he didn't deserve. Even if we appealed and won, where would Jim go to get his reputation back?

What galled me was that Judge Gordon had to know he was forcing us to settle. Months earlier, Judge Gordon had overruled my motion to dismiss, basing his decision on the lack of an Ohio Supreme Court adoption of the law of judgmental immunity in Ohio. Now, he did an about-face, announcing that one unreported, obscure appellate decision—not even in the appellate jurisdiction of his court—was the law in Ohio, despite the absence of an Ohio Supreme Court ruling. Judge Gordon left us no choice. Either we settled, or we tried convincing the jury that the law the judge told them applied to this case somehow didn't apply to Jim Glass.

What can a lawyer do when judges lack the aptitude to manage a complex case, which, in civil litigation, happens frequently in state courts? The only forum in Ohio to voice concerns about the *quality* of judges is the ballot box. And in this corner of democracy, the citizenry votes in ignorance. Voters know little about a trial judge's aptitude for work ethic, unbiased judgment, and decisiveness in the stressful environment of big-stakes litigation in civil cases.[2]

In state court, some judges fail to meet the criteria of an ideal judge: one that encompasses *objectivity* (an open mind), *judicial temperament* (a healthy portion of patience and the capacity to refrain from getting ticked off at droning lawyers), *legal knowledge* (proficiency in substantive law, evidence, and procedure), and *quality decisions* (backed up by courtroom experience and sound legal reasoning).

The idea that three years of law school and six or even ten years of law practice qualifies a lawyer for judicial office, especially a trial judge, makes no sense to experienced trial attorneys. And don't be fooled by a

2. The Brennan Center for Justice at NYU School of Law has recently released Choosing State Judges: A Plan for Reform. This report of a three-year research project urges states to replace state supreme court elections with an appointment system, to increase public accountability and to eliminate reelection pressure, dark money, and politically influenced appointments by appointing state supreme court justices to a long (but single) term.

judge or lawyers with 20 years experience, they may have stopped learning after their first year. Yet, we are muted by the fear of allegations of unethical conduct. Any public criticism of judicial competence is lumped into an attack on the independence and integrity of the judicial system—or sour grapes.

Today, judges' salaries are too low to attract the best lawyers to run for judicial office. Our Founding Fathers understood that the integrity of the legal system depended on independent, fair-minded judges. Ohio's political system of attracting and electing quality candidates to fill the position of a trial judge falls short of what the Founders had in mind. Yet once a politically driven or inexperienced lawyer is elected, trial lawyers must suffer in silence. I can deal with abusive lawyers; I may complain about naïve juries, though most of the time juries get it right. But I accept their verdicts; even those that ignore the realities of the disease process. I am up to the challenge of discrediting experts for hire, but I'm powerless against judges who take sides. An appeal to a higher court because a judge exercised poor judgment, legally defined as an *abuse of discretion*, is a costly exercise in futility.

This is speculation on my part, but I suspect that Judge Gordon knew he would be reversed by the appellate judges for multiple rulings prior and during trial. If he forced a settlement, there would be no appeal. And there wasn't.

28 The Barrister Wore Lipstick

Lesson 28: Confident women trial lawyers are assertive and let men know they won't be pushed around.

It was 9:00 in the evening after the fourth day of trial. I was in my home office working on my direct examination of our expert pulmonologist scheduled to testify the next day. My phone rang. The shrill voice on the other end of the phone made it clear: "We are going to lose this case." That afternoon, while conducting a direct examination of one of our expert witnesses, I had misstated one of the many laboratory reports in the plaintiff's medical record. The lab test I quoted as normal was above the normal range. Embarrassed, I listened and apologized. The phone call lasted two minutes.

I had been with the law firm for a little over a year. The managing partner had asked me to assist Maryellen Spirito in trial. I would sit second chair, meaning I would assist Maryellen, rather than take the lead in managing the evidence and witnesses. I'd had more experience in the courtroom than Maryellen, but not in the defense of doctors. Maryellen had been a nurse before entering law school. In this lawsuit, she knew the medicine leading up to the death of a kidney transplant patient better than me and better than anyone else in the case, even better than the doctors we represented.

When I hung up the phone, I was a little taken aback. Given my experience in the courtroom, I didn't believe one misquoted value would torpedo our defense of the doctors. I decided I could finish my prep for my next witness early tomorrow morning. I turned on the TV in the living room and plopped down on the couch to relax a bit before turning in. I found a rerun of *My Cousin Vinny*. I've watched this movie many times. Besides the humorous Italian macho that I was familiar with growing up near Buffalo, the prosecutor's textbook opening statement had been referenced many times in continuing education classes as an example of a tight factual summary and persuasive presentation without arguing the prosecution's case.

The phone rang again; it was 11 p.m.

The passage of two hours had no calming effect on Maryellen. My mistake, I was told a second time, could cost us the case.

I put on my jeans and a sweatshirt and drove to our downtown office 15 minutes from my home, barged in, scared the hell out of the cleaning people, found the three-ring binders stuffed with medical records from Ohio State, and searched for the lab studies and test leading up to Sharon Smiley's kidney transplant. I did get the lab value wrong, but my immediate reaction was that this lab test was too insignificant in the milieu of voluminous medical data that supported our theory of the cause of Sharon Smiley's death to hurt our defense. Driving back home, I thought Maryellen was stressed out and overreacting. However, I would soon learn that she was a perfectionist and intensely competitive. Her oft-repeated mantra, "Know everything," is a nearly impossible goal for trial lawyers. Yet, she carried that mindset to every case she was assigned. When I became the managing partner of our boutique medical and legal malpractice law firm, former clients often requested Maryellen to be their lawyer. I knew, and our doctor clients (some of them cocky surgeons) knew, they were in good hands.

Maryellen grew up in New Jersey. Most everyone from New Jersey can't or won't say their "Rs" like the rest of us, except people from Boston. Instead of Jerry she calls me JAHREEE. Before law school she worked as a psychiatric nurse, helping patients with mental health problems. Maryellen's skills as a psych nurse would show up in the courtroom. She was in her early 30s by the time she graduated from the Ohio State University School of Law in 1983.

Maryellen's pinball path to our office had more to do with her medical knowledge than a glass ceiling. In the early 80s, female trial attorneys were seen and not heard. They were outsiders. Maryellen's challenges were different than mine. I had mentors, a lawyer that took me under his wing and showed me what to do and what not to do. Her first job was with a small defense firm. Luckily, this firm employed lawyers that distinguished themselves in the defense of physicians. Maryellen's medical knowledge was an indispensable resource that punched her ticket to the courtroom. She had the opportunity to work and learn from competent trial lawyers, though occasionally the fact that she was a woman in a male-dominated profession would slap her in the face.

When she was hired at her first job, the managing partner told her not to shut her door so he could just yell her name when he needed her. She noticed the other lawyers in the firm worked with their doors closed. Within a few weeks, she accompanied a senior lawyer to a pretrial. When she was introduced to the judge, he said, "Jesus, not another girl lawyer." Most of the lawyers she worked with and against were men. She endured gender bias with grace, though she came into my office one day and told me, "Men are so stupid." This made me squirm in my chair; the last time I looked, I had all the trappings of a man. I have to confess that I have been guilty of obnoxious behavior involving women. But once you're married and have a daughter, the jokes aren't so funny. I recall a story she told me about an interview with a defense firm many years ago. The interview had gone well. Just before she got up to leave, the managing partner asked if she was married and what her husband did. She asked him why he asked such a question. Maryellen said his response had to do with how much they had to pay her. Married women would need less money, he said. She walked out.

There was an incident in one of our cases, though, that made me angry. Maryellen was in a pretrial with opposing counsel. The reason for the pretrial was to see if the case could be settled. However, the insurance company had not approved money to settle out of court. The plaintiff's attorney got angry and as they were leaving the courthouse, he threatened to throw her down the stairway. I wanted to report the lawyer's threats to the judge or file an ethics complaint, but Maryellen snuffed the idea. My sense of it was that she internalized this male behavior by committing to kicking the lawyer's ass in the courtroom, which she did regularly.

Very few lawyers I know achieved the skills necessary to become a go-to trial attorney without a mentor. Maryellen had a unique training ground. She had a medical background. She was a psych nurse and before she went to law school she earned a master's degree in social work at Ohio State. One of her invisible traits was her ability to read the room. Besides the sporadic help on how to do it, she picked up trial skills quickly. It helped that she was in her 30s when she entered the practice of law, but what else made her different from the average associate lawyer early in her career? She brought valuable insight to the table when she was added to the trial team. Maryellen understood the interrelationship between the patient, the doctor, and the difference between complications and negligence. She proved rather quickly that she could articulate the difference between an unavoidable complication and a breach of the standard of care to people on a jury without medical knowledge. Trust me on this one: Many so-called experienced trial lawyers need to be told what not do, but not her. Maryellen could be assertive without being a bitch. She had an edge to her personality, but she had a light touch when it was needed. Before she joined our law firm, she had been with five different firms. After her first job in a law firm, many opportunities landed on her doorstep. She would finish a trial or deposition and weeks later, she'd get a call from opposing counsel asking, "Hey, how would you like to join our firm?"

Maryellen worked in our firm for 18 years. During that time we had between seven and eight trial lawyers in the firm, not all of them the first choice of the insurance companies that paid our fees. Often when a case would not settle and a trial date was weeks away, I would get a call from a senior claims lawyer and ask me if a particular lawyer was going to try a case by himself, meaning the company lacked confidence in that lawyer's abilities. I never got a call from claims personnel asking whether Maryellen was going to handle a trial by herself.

Before Gayle Arnold hired me as a partner, most of my practice focused on suing doctors and hospitals, except for a few legal malpractice cases. When I finished reviewing Mrs. Smiley's medical records, I told Maryellen this case should be settled. I had read in the medical records and the depositions that Mrs. Smiley, age 48, needed a kidney transplant. After surgery, she had multiple urinary tract infections and required a nephrostomy tube (a catheter inserted in the kidney to drain urine). After a year of frequent infections and nephrostomy tube exchanges, she was taken to surgery. The surgeon found a silk suture loosely wrapped around one of the two ureters (muscular tubes that transfer urine to the bladder). The plaintiffs claimed that the sutured ureter caused the backflow of urine, resulting in infection, kidney damage, and death.

Maryellen's defense focused on the lack of causation. Our experts would testify that at the time of surgery, the defendant discovered a very poor native vasculature (small atherosclerotic arteries) supplying blood to the kidney. This condition prolonged the time to perform the transplant, which extended time of lack of reperfusion of blood and led to warming the donor kidney. As time ticked away, the awaiting donor kidney was permanently damaged. True, a silk suture was found around the ureter, but Maryellen would argue that the unexpected lengthy surgery was the true cause of kidney failure and death.

A suture around the ureter shouldn't be there, and we couldn't argue it was a complication of the procedure. Can there be anything worse than an inexcusable surgical error? Yes—in this lawsuit, a righteous witness speaking his mind. That righteous witness was the patient's treating doctor and a colleague of the defendant voicing his criticisms of our client under oath. Holy crap. Our client had done a poor job of responding to Mrs. Smiley's nephrologist's inquiries on the need for follow up. When our client wrote a letter to Mrs. Smiley terminating his medical care because further surgery wasn't necessary, the treating nephrologist got mad. He testified that our client abandoned Mrs. Smiley. This testimony would explode like a landmine in the courtroom. If the jury hated our client, Maryellen had no chance of winning this case.

Winning the case required damage control. Maryellen, like any first-chair lawyer, would take on the most damaging witnesses in the case. When she cross-examined the nephrologist, she unobtrusively got the nephrologist to acknowledge that Mrs. Smiley unfortunately had advanced atherosclerotic disease; that was the reason her kidney stopped functioning in the first place. Not only were the arteries to her kidney compromised, but so were the arteries elsewhere in the body, such as her heart and her brain. When she showed the nephrologist and the jury that Mrs. Smiley had suffered a stroke as a result of her advanced sclerosis of the arteries in her brain, it appeared entirely reasonable to cancel the anticipated reimplantation surgery. It would have been a futile effort to implant a new kidney in the long run, and high-risk in the short run. The jury agreed and found in favor of our defendants.

When Maryellen got into her mid-60s, the thought of retiring came into her mind, as was typical for most trial lawyers. It's the stress that trial lawyers internalize that starts to tire the mind and affect concentration. Trial work takes stamina, and stamina may be hard to find when trial lawyers age into their 60s. But there is another problem. When a trial lawyer is respected by their peers, and judges openly compliment their professionalism and competence, and they know how challenging it is to acquire the effective skills of a trial lawyer, it's like the force of gravity. It's hard to pull away from that feeling—a combination of aristocracy and elitism. Hand a lawyer a microphone and you'll hear them start to talk about the cases they've won. It's painful for a lawyer to surrender what's so hard to come by. And for some of us, we came from a background of anonymity. Maybe you scored the winning touchdown in a high school football game or were an all-conference goalie in field hockey. But in college and law school, only your friends know your name. Success as a trial lawyer engenders a sense of strength, the power of knowing you can help people that are down and lift a burden from their shoulders that they cannot do without your help. That identity as a unique, powerful individual is hard to give up. But when the feeling is gone, it's time to take down the sheepskin.

I remember the day Maryellen stood in the doorway of my office just hours after winning another high-stress case, and announced she was done trying cases. The judge was good ole Judge Gordon. According to Maryellen, the judge favored the plaintiff's lawyer with his rulings throughout the trial and at least once berated her in front of the jury. "I'm done with this shit," she said. The trial involved Dr. Muller, a cardiologist and principal investigator for an experimental device called the Watchman. It's a small, parachute-shaped device designed to plug a small sac or out-pouch coming off the upper left chamber of the heart, called the left atrial appendage (LAA). The LAA acts as a reservoir when the blood pressure in the heart is high. Unfortunately, sometimes when people have atrial fibrillation, an irregular heartbeat, blood will clot in the out-pouch. Clots that form in the LAA can travel to the brain and cause a stroke. Before the Watchman device, patients with A-fib were put on a strong blood thinner, which was not ideal, and even dangerous.

When Dr. Muller signed up Mr. Blake, age 76, for this experimental procedure and placed him into a nationwide randomized study, Mr. Blake signed a 15-page consent form that laid out every risk associated with placement of the device, including the risk of air bubbles introduced into the venous system during the procedure—an air embolus—blocking flow of blood to the brain, causing a stroke. During Mr. Blake's procedure, air leaked into a vein and caused a stroke. After the procedure, Dr. Muller went to Mr. Blake's hospital room to tell him he had a stroke. His 51-year-old son said, "I guess these things can happen." Dr. Muller shifted his gaze to Mr. Blake. "Not to me," he said. Mr. Blake died months later. The son thought something must have gone wrong. The family sued.

Some might say the trial judge assigned to this case was as sharp as a marble. Not me, though. I'd say that despite his experience, he wasn't suited for complex litigation and had a tendency to take sides. In one of the most bizarre decisions ever by a trial judge, he allowed the plaintiff's attorney to put his expert on the witness stand to give testimony before the Maryellen gave the jury her opening statement—unheard of, and an obvious show of favoritism. The expert was only available the first day of the trial. Either the trial should have been continued, or the plaintiff forced to play a video presentation of the witness's testimony at the appropriate time in the plaintiff's case—an omen of things to come. During the trial, Maryellen called Mr. Blake's wife and three adult children, who confirmed that they had no doubt their father read every word in the consent form. The plaintiff's counsel sensed that the jury was favoring the doctor. A series of objections started. Maryellen would stand up to respond to the objections. "Sit down," the trial judge repeatedly told her. But when her male co-counsel assisting her at trial responded to objections, the judge would listen intently to his argument.

During Maryellen's final argument, plaintiff's counsel objected numerous times. Experienced lawyers rarely ever do this unless something is said to a jury that is extremely prejudicial. As I described early in this book, in the case I tried against Charlie Brown, the interruption causes the speaker to lose their concentration. The plaintiff's lawyer here knew that he could get away with disrupting Maryellen's final argument, so he did it with impunity. Despite the shenanigans, the jury found in favor of Dr. Muller. Today the Watchman procedure has a reported success rate of 94 percent.

Later that day, Maryellen appeared in my doorway. She said she would stay with the firm, but she preferred to assist other lawyers in putting the cases together and taking depositions of tough experts. Her peers, years ago, had voted her into the list of Best Lawyers in America. She knew she was respected by the small group of elite lawyers competent to try a medical malpractice case. She never told me her exact reasons for begging off trials. But I think the blatant lack of respect from a trial judge that knew better made her angry, and why should she face a sexist judge when she didn't have to?

Recently, I asked Maryellen what advice she would give to a young female lawyer. She said, "Always be prepared, and don't let men push you around."

That's Maryellen.

29 The Search Satisfaction Error that Ruined a Doctor's Life

Lesson 29: Complex evidence such as medicine and science may be counterintuitive to common sense, and simplistic courtroom presentations are often misleading. Be ready to illustrate the facts that your opponent ignored.

Three hours after Louise Franklin's[1] arrival in the ICU, a doctor ordered a large dose of fentanyl and sedatives, then removed her ventilator and life support. She died within minutes.

Two years later, a scorching headline in the local newspaper declared: "[P]hysician allegedly ordered 28 people potentially fatal doses of opioid painkillers. Their families wonder why he wasn't stopped."

A news article quoting the newly elected state attorney general stoked the fury of the plaintiffs and their attorneys: "It looks like we've got a serial killer on the loose with a medical license and access to fentanyl."

Two months earlier, Mid Town Hospital officials, in the mistaken belief that transparency would bring about a quick and reasonable solution of claims against the hospital, notified the families of 34 ICU patients

1. Except for the criminal defense lawyers and Greg Foliano, all other names in this chapter have been changed.

that Dr. Oscar Beacon gave "significantly excessive and potentially fatal dosages" of fentanyl that "hastened the death of their family member." No one understood why he used higher amounts of painkillers for palliative care on terminal patients until after his criminal trial. Soon Dr. Beacon would become known as "Doctor Death."

Sonic booms thundered across the city's skyline as the plaintiff's lawyers broke the sound barrier racing to the courthouse, filing medical malpractice cases against the hospital and Dr. Beacon. The local television stations and media outlets began running interviews of the family members of the deceased patients and their lawyers.

Sonny Spees, an experienced and respected medical malpractice lawyer, represented Oliver Franklin, whose wife died in the ICU less than 30 minutes after Dr. Beacon gave her comfort care—healthcare intended to provide support and comfort to patients close to death. On the day after filing a lawsuit, Mr. Franklin, flanked by his lawyer, gave an interview to a local journalist. "They killed her," he said. The article reported that Mr. Franklin's lawsuit stated that Beacon told Mr. Franklin that his wife was brain dead. This allegation suddenly spread to other plaintiff's lawsuits. The article highlighted the more damning allegations made during the interview: ". . . What [Oliver Frankin] didn't know was Beacon had the excessive fentanyl administered five minutes *before* the two talked about removing life-support . . . , the hospital's records show, Spees said," And not to be missed, attorney Spees' allegation: "The excessive dosage was grossly inappropriate given [her] condition and was either ordered negligently and not properly reviewed or was intentionally prescribed by Dr. Beacon for the purpose of ending [her] life." Eager for sound bites, the press caused a plaintiff's lawyer feeding frenzy for the spotlight as they lured new clients.

Soon thereafter, another article entitled "System Failure" quoted plaintiff's lawyers, claiming the hospital's oversight policies were insufficient to prevent overdoses. The hospital, of course, was a deep pocket; thus plaintiff's lawyers hammered them relentlessly in the press. "[T] he attention being afforded the deaths will likely save lives across the country," Mr. Spees stated. Mr. Franklin expressed his deep regret over his decision to remove life support. "Beacon," he said, "had told him his wife was 'brain dead, heart dead, and lung dead." What the press failed to realize was that the plaintiff's lawyers were posturing. When lawyers speak publicly about their cases, they talk about the facts that build on the theories that support their claims. Unfavorable facts are ignored or denied. The plaintiff's lawyer did not mention that these so-called victims were at the end of life, suffering from organ failure, or that many could only live on life support.

In an earlier article, a professor of medicine and critical care specialist at a major midwestern university hospital claimed: "To give 1,000 (micrograms) is so far above and beyond what we would ever give that it is clear there the intent is to accelerate the death," meaning Dr. Beacon intended to kill the patient. Later, he would appear as an expert for the prosecution in the Beacon murder trial.

As the malpractice cases against Beacon became the stuff of murder, driven by the plaintiff's lawyers posturing in the media at every opportunity, the case took on the popularity of a binge-worthy TV crime drama. As the settlement values of the unresolved malpractice cases catapulted to astronomical numbers, the plaintiff's attorneys ramped up their characterization of their lawsuits as instruments for public good, meaning their goal was to improve medical care. Another local newspaper quoted one of the family attorneys: "Still, in these types of cases, . . . clients aren't focused on a payout. I've never had a client who didn't say 'I want to bring a case because I don't want anybody to go through what I went through. I want to make a difference.' . . . The biggest concern now, Mr. Spees said, is how this could happen to 27 families."

I spent the first half of my career as a plaintiff's lawyer suing doctors and hospitals, getting paid under a contingent fee contract. Reading some of the comments in the newspapers reminded me of many initial meetings with potential clients wanting to sue a physician. At some point in the conversation, the angry and grieving family member would say that they wanted to make sure what happened to their family member didn't happen to someone else, and at least make certain the doctor lost his license. I empathized with my clients, but I learned early on that a frank discussion about client expectations was necessary before a contingent fee contract was signed. I would tell these potential clients that the only thing I could do for them if I filed a medical malpractice case was sue for money. "If you're expecting me to go after the doctor's license or change the way a doctor practices medicine," I would say, "that may happen in the short term, but fear of litigation rarely improves medical care." I told my potential clients I would be spending thousands of dollars of my own money for advanced cost, which they would have to pay back, and only if we won would I get a percentage of the money recovered—usually 40 percent, the standard fee in malpractice cases. I truly do not recall any client in a case I lost having the resources to reimburse me for $25,000 to $75,000 of litigation cost. I'd tell potential clients, "If you really want to strip a doctor of his license or prevent bad medical practice, you will have to pay me a retainer and an hourly rate so that we can file a complaint and gather evidence to submit to the medical board." In the 21 years I did plaintiff's litigation, I never had a client say to me, "OK, Mr. Todaro, forget this contingent fee business, I'll pay your retainer and hourly rate and all the advance cost of litigation up front."

Imperfect human performance is an inherent and unavoidable element of the human condition, especially in the complex and uncertain environment of medicine. Mistakes are made, and lawsuits capitalize on these inevitable mistakes. If lawsuits change behavior in medicine, it is short-lived. Medical research and evidence-based medicine are what move the needle toward better healthcare practices, not malpractice lawsuits. No matter how perfectly we design a system to guide human performance, human failure is one of life's constants. True victims of malpractice deserve compensation, but after decades of trying malpractice cases, unavoidable bad outcomes are mistaken for malpractice. And after decades of reviewing medical cases, very few of them are legitimate malpractice cases. But medical experts for hire are smart and are not intimidated; there are only a few medical decisions that cannot be second guessed.

***

Oscar Beacon peered at the computer screen in the nurse's station displaying Louise Franklin's long history of medical problems. She had been admitted to the hospital for breathing problems twice that month and she had coughed up blood in the ambulance on the way to the hospital; her heart stopped twice. In the emergency room, her heart stopped three more times. The doctors pounded her chest and shot her up with atropine and epinephrine, heart drugs that constrict blood vessels and stimulate the heart to pump more forcefully. The emergency room doctor inserted a tube in her chest to relieve a large tension pneumothorax—a bubble of air squeezing her heart, caused by CPR forceful enough to break a few ribs. Despite CPR, her heartbeat was too slow and irregular.

The emergency room doctor placed two pacing pads on her chest near her heart to deliver a controlled pulse of electrical current that would regulate the conduction pathways and contraction of the heart. The pulse sequence was set for 70 beats a minute to maintain an adequate heart rate and cardiac output. The EMS crew and the ER doctors had saved her life five times, but without the external pacemaker, a fatal arrythmia would ensue. If she were to have any chance of survival, she needed to go to the ICU immediately.

Louise Franklin was 67 years old, retired, had been a smoker, and had struggled to breathe for years. Lately, her portable oxygen tank wasn't helping. When EMS arrived at her home, her husband said, "We've been through this before; she's had a heart attack, COPD, congestive heart failure, and a stroke." Her medical record warned she had stage 4 kidney failure, which prevented her emergency room doctors from ordering an imaging study with opaque contrast to evaluate the function of her heart. This was her third COPD exacerbation in a month—airway inflammation and fluid in the lungs impaired her breathing. Louise's body was playing a dangerous game of Russian roulette.

When Mr. Franklin was allowed to see his wife, he was horrified. Her chest muscles continuously spasmed from the shocks of the external pacemaker. Louise was in a perpetual state of jerking and twitching movements. He couldn't bear to look any longer—only hours ago, they were in their living room having a normal conversation. Stunned, he wondered how this could happen. An ICU nurse paged the in-house crisis ministry pastor.

The chaplain escorted Mr. Franklin to a quiet room near the ICU. Dr. Beacon came in and explained that Louise had had multiple cardiac arrests, and respiratory and kidney failure. Later, Mr. Franklin would recall Dr. Beacon saying her organs were dead. Dr. Beacon would deny using such draconian language in his discussions with families at the bedside. He would testify that he made sure Mr. Franklin understood that only the ventilator, pacer, and vasopressors—strong heart stimulation drugs, were keeping her alive. When she arrived in the ICU, the nurses had temporarily removed the pacing pads to see if her heart would beat on its own, but her pulse dipped dangerously into the 40s. They tried a second time, with the same result. When critically ill patients teeter on the edge of death, the expression "the wolf is at the door" echoes in the hallways of ICUs. When the heart falters, jackals drool and show their fangs.

Mr. Franklin could not understand why she declined so rapidly. In the quiet room, options were discussed. There were only two: continue the breathing machine, heart drugs, and pacer, or remove all life support and provide comfort care so she would not feel any pain as she died. One of Dr. Beacon's qualities, according to the nurses, was his caring bedside manner in explaining palliative care to families of stricken patients. Few people are prepared or have given a thought about making end-of-life decisions for a parent or a spouse. It's our nature to believe that doctors surely can do more to make things better. After 50 years, I have come to the reality that many diseases are unforgiving, and most of us naïvely assume a pill or surgery will restore our health like nothing ever happened. After a discussion of the options, Dr. Beacon asked Mr. Franklin, "What is the decision your wife would make in this situation?"

Overcome by anger and grief, Mr. Franklin started pounding the walls. The two nurses and the chaplain finally got him to take a breath and calmed him enough that he could go back to see his wife. As the husband stood near the bedside of his unconscious wife, seeing her on a breathing machine, watching her body twitch and quiver, Dr. Beacon recalls him saying, "She wouldn't want this; take it all away."

Unfortunately, neither Dr. Beacon nor the nurses documented the short conversation with Mr. Franklin about her fatal condition or options of care. The lack of documentation of important conversations around risk and benefits of treatment is an invitation to hop on the conveyer belt leading directly to the courtroom.

Dr. Beacon ordered 600 mcg of fentanyl and 6 mg of Versed to be given to Mrs. Franklin for palliative care. These were much higher doses than given by many doctors providing comfort care. In his deposition, he would testify that it was *his* practice to provide full pain relief upfront, rather than give smaller amounts and wait to see if the patient needed more after life support was removed. The former approach was typically how comfort care is given. Dr. Beacon believed that chasing pain instead of preventing it was not the best medicine.

Fentanyl is a pain killer 100 times more potent than morphine and is commonly used by anesthesiologists during surgery, and Versed is a sedative. Both drugs were given to Mrs. Franklin at 11:23 p.m. The ventilator was removed at 11:28. At 11:53 p.m., September 30th, 2018, two hours and six minutes after she was admitted to the ICU, Louise Franklin was pronounced dead. Dr. Beacon's recommendation to remove life support and provide comfort care in less than two hours would put a target on his back. Normally, less than 500 mcg of fentanyl and 1 or 2 mg of Versed is used in this setting. But in Dr. Beacon's mind, that amount would not ensure his patient did not suffer during the process of dying. He had this view because, unlike most intensivists in an ICU, Dr. Beacon completed a residency in anesthesia at a major medical research hospital.

Mid Town Hospital used an automated medication system that required orders for all prescription drugs. In-house pharmacists would review and approve the orders and advise on the safe usage of drugs, checking dosages and efficacy of drug therapy. During the investigation, it became clear that nurses were commonly overriding the system to obtain medications for the ICU more quickly. And it became obvious that many, but not all, of the drugs used in Dr. Beacon's palliative comfort care practice were obtained by override and without prior pharmacy approval. We would learn that Dr. Beacon knew nothing about how the drugs were obtained.

An emergency order allowed the nurses to speed up the delivery of powerful pain medications to expedite palliative care for patients lingering on life support with no chance of survival. However, the prosecutor's office thought otherwise. If a patient was sedated while on life support, there was no emergency, or an emergent need to give a patient massive doses of painkillers. Ducking system warnings and pharmacist oversight meant that Beacon intended to end a patient's life without getting caught, the prosecutors would tell the jury.

Despite the plaintiff's attorneys claim that lawsuits change hospital practices for the better, the hospital had begun changing their system of dispensing medication long before any lawsuits were filed. One thing the lawsuits did for sure, though, was to embarrass otherwise competent doctors and nurses practicing at the hospital. Malpractice lawsuits mark the defendant doctor as incompetent, and doctors and hospitals fear litigation because of the loss of prestige from years of toil and hard-earned validation. As expected, the plaintiff's attorneys would use this embarrassment to leverage their settlement values.

Four months after the hospital released patient records to the county prosecutor, Dr. Beacon was indicted on 25 counts of murder. "I have found no one, nowhere," the prosecutor explained in local TV news interviews, "that says 500 micrograms of fentanyl is an appropriate use of fentanyl for treatment of somebody being taken off a ventilator. . . . A dosage at that level could not support any legitimate medical purpose and the dosage at that level would cause someone's death." Of course, months before the prosecutor's indictments, headlines from the local press had unwittingly orchestrated a narrative of a "killer in the nighttime ICU."

When malpractice cases blitzed the hospital, the hospital administrators turned to Greg Foliano to represent Dr. Beacon. Under Oscar

Beacon's contract, the hospital was obligated to hire a lawyer to provide him with a defense. Foliano had defended childbirth injury claims against hospitals and on behalf of major malpractice insurance companies. These lawsuits are the most intensive, medically complex, and stressful cases in the cottage industry of brain-damaged baby litigation.

Foliano stands six-foot-two and could likely still wrestle in his weight class at the college level. His fierce competitive edge sometimes has a bite. Listening to him prep obstetricians and neonatologists for trial is like attending a medical conference of leading physicians in reproductive medicine. He would read textbooks and gather all the medical literature on the alleged missed diagnosis and the medical illness involved before he met with his medical experts. He inhales medical knowledge, and armed with facts and statistics, he often exposes the faulty opinions of his adversaries.

Foliano was hired to defend Dr. Beacon in the civil malpractice cases, but the hospital's statements to the families and the press cuffed his hands behind his back. They wanted the cases settled. But after Foliano's thorough review of the records, he thought the cases were easily defensible. Myself and others in the office that worked behind the scenes agreed. Foliano handed out rolls of duct tape to ensure that everyone in the office kept their mouths shut. There would be no public comments, despite the plaintiff's lawyer's continuous bashing of Beacon in local news articles. Dr. Beacon's criminal defense lawyers handled responses to inquiries from the local press, but in true defense lawyer fashion, they revealed little. Plaintiff's lawyers fed the local press a steady stream of self-serving sound bites. Nearly every week, it seemed like an episode of *Murder, She Wrote*. The vision of overdosed ICU patients marinated in the city for months leading up to the trial.

Another tactic that played out on the giant chessboard of gamesmanship involved media releases of just plain dirt—the kind of dirt that won't rub off. One of the newspaper editors was intrigued by the two-year gap in Beacon's resume. He started digging. "As a college student, Beacon had with another young man built a pipe bomb in a dorm room and used it to blow up a trash can on campus. Federal investigators said Beacon then tried to frame someone else for the crime by planting bomb-making materials in that person's car. Ultimately, Beacon pleaded guilty in the case and was sentenced to six months in federal prison."

The plaintiffs, hearing this news, pointed to Beacon's criminal conviction as undeniable proof of negligent hiring by the hospital. And of course, overdosing patients with intent to kill made perfect sense given Beacon's criminal mind.

In criminal cases, unlike civil cases, the defendant's right against self-incrimination prevents the prosecutor from calling the defendant to the witness stand. In civil cases, though, the plaintiff may force the defendant to testify, and often they do, attempting to elicit favorable concessions from the lips of the defendant. Revealing a defendant's past demeaning misbehavior or revealing a moral defect is a particularly popular tactic, and an effective one. The more the jury dislikes a party in the courtroom, the more likely they are to punish the undeserving.

The plaintiffs dug further into the federal prosecutor's files for details of the pipe bomb. They subpoenaed Dr. Beacon's medical board application and medical school applications to see if he disclosed his convictions. They wanted evaluations of his performance during his residency training. In his medical school application, under the list of extracurricular activities, he had said he was a walk-on for a major college basketball team. He had been on scholarship for the basketball team at his previous college before the pipe bomb indictment. At the beginning of the basketball season, the new team held a tryout for basketball players who would fill the role of practice fodder. Beacon's name appeared on the list that designated the walk-ons that made the team. He was never called to participate in any practices and the list was lost with the passage of time. However, the plaintiff's attorneys were convinced he lied on his resume.

The plaintiffs hunted for any other examples of wrongdoing as evidence of flawed character. Dr. Beacon would deny he told Mr. Franklin his wife was brain dead, heart dead, and lung dead, but the plaintiff's lawyers intended to construct an image of a habitual liar. The jury should not believe anything he said.

When the parties filed motions on the numerous issues in the case, the press called Foliano asking for a comment. He either ignored the call or said no comment. However, Foliano's method of communicating with the press involved embedding precise details of the deceased patient's terminal condition in his responsive pleadings. He knew the local press was monitoring the court docket looking for information. On the few occasions the local newspapers would quote Foliano's information about the patients' hopeless medical prognosis, usually Greg's description was buried in the article. We attributed these slights to the persistent negativity bias of the press toward the so-called killer doctor. And, of course, crime sells.

During the pendency of the criminal case, it became painfully clear that a couple of plaintiffs were highly motivated to assist the prosecutor. As the criminal trial date neared, the prosecutor disclosed their extensive list of witnesses. One of their medical witnesses was a physician named Melvin Switzer. Mr. Spees had used Switzer to sign the obligatory affidavit of merit in Louise Franklin's malpractice lawsuit. An affidavit of merit shows that a lawsuit has been preliminarily reviewed by a qualified doctor who believes the standard of care was breached. Since the prosecutor's office had no lawyers with any experience in taking a medical malpractice case to trial, Dr. Switzer's appearance on the prosecutor's witness list meant to us that the plaintiffs were feeding experts to the prosecutor's office. Dr. Switzer was a leading figure in the lucrative business of testifying. Since 2005, in our database alone, he has shown up as a plaintiff's expert witness in more than 20 cases.

Another tactic by the plaintiff's lawyers used to help the prosecutor's office was immediately filing on the court docket depositions of hospital employees and treating doctors taken in the medical malpractice cases. Depostions of witnesses are rarely filed until just before a civil case is going to trial, not years before. The filings made the depositions open to anyone who wanted to read what was said. If the prosecutor's office monitored the civil dockets, they would see the filings and have access to information they otherwise would not have. Whether overtly or secretly assisting the prosecutor, the plaintiffs wanted a conviction. A guilty verdict would drive up the settlement value of their cases.

Foliano, of course, was not sitting idly in his office watching the gamesmanship play out. The defense counsel for Beacon in the criminal case, Jose Baez and Diane Menashe, were experienced criminal defense lawyers. Jose Baez had successfully represented high-profile defendants Casey Anthony and Aaron Hernandez. Diane Menashe is one of the most sought-after criminal defense lawyers in the city. Diane would occasionally discuss cross-examination of the prosecution's medical witnesses with Greg. Menashe proved to be a quick study, highly unusual for lawyers with no background in medicine tasked with cross-examining hardened medical experts in medical malpractice cases. According to Foliano, her cross-exanimations were sharp and effective. This is high praise from Foliano; Trust me on this, he is not easily impressed. There are occasions in our office when we've worked together on cases, and after reading one of my depositions of a plaintiff's expert, he has been heard yelling, "Hey, genius? I can't work with this."

The criminal trial took six weeks to conclude. It was interesting to follow the daily commentary of close to 2,000 people viewing the trial on the Law and Crime network. Trial lawyers instinctively know that if the jury doesn't like you or your client, you're on a slippery slope. On average, two out of three court watchers were critical of the plaintiff's families and the prosecutor. Some expressed the opinion that the families appeared to overreact emotionally to the loss of family members who had suffered severe disabling diseases, were unable to survive without life support, and would have died anyway.

In closing arguments, it was reported that the prosecutors relied on a law school example of a vivid illustration of intent to kill in a murder case. The prosecutor told the jury that if a man jumped off a building intending to commit suicide, but was shot and killed on the way down, it's still murder. This would be a correct statement in a criminal case; however, the prosecutor didn't understand what malpractice lawyers know from years of experience. Suing a doctor for failing to properly treat a patient in circumstances where the natural course of the disease will eventually take the patient's life, whether immediately or within a few years, is a case with a high mortality rate in the courtroom.

"Proximate cause" is an essential element in injury claims. The concept encapsulates the logic of cause and effect. It's called the "but for" test—but for the negligence of the defendant, the injury or death would not have occurred. For example, say a plaintiff's family sues a building owner because their father fell down a stairwell and died, and negligence was proven because of a lack of handrails. But an autopsy showed the father had a large brain aneurysm that bled, causing elevated intracranial pressure and loss of consciousness, and was the likely cause of his fall. Negligence was proven, but not causation. The man did not fall because of the lack of handrails. He fell to his death because he became unconscious from a fatal brain bleed.

Essentially, the idiom "no harm, no foul" springs from a common belief that we hold people responsible for the actual damage caused for improper conduct, not what could have happened. Despite arguments claiming that fentanyl and strong sedatives killed the 14 so-called victims, the medical records documented that many of the deceased plaintiffs could not live without life support and died from the severely disabling and ravaging diseases that initially brought them to the ICU. Despite the lack of documentation of Dr. Beacon's end-of-life discussions with family members, there was enough evidence in the records to satisfy jurors that the discussions took place. Despite the families claiming they had no idea Beacon would give excessive doses of fentanyl to hasten a painless death, Foliano felt that the jury would conclude no family member not thinking of a payout would refuse to consent to give whatever was necessary to avoid the risk of a painful death, regardless of the amount of painkillers used.

The jury exonerated Dr. Beacon on all 14 counts.

***

When Foliano first introduced me to Dr. Beacon, I sensed something was off. His body moved like a robot. When we shook hands, his right hand was claw-like and his grip felt like shaking hands with a frail, elderly man. When I watched him walk in the hallways in our office, his gait reminded me of a stroke patient. Later, he was diagnosed with post-traumatic stress disorder. Oscar Beacon is now 50 years old, a well-trained intensivist with no self-esteem, no income, no prospects of ever being employed, suffering from PTSD, and shunned by those who believe he beat the rap. How did this happen?

A good place to start is research by academic radiologists, studying why radiologists miss what seems like an obvious abnormality (in hindsight) on X-rays, CT scans, and MRIs. As discussed in an earlier chapter, researchers identified one type of mental mistake called "search satisfaction errors." This error occurs when radiologists stop searching for subsequent abnormalities on an X-ray after finding the initial one and fail to complete their search. It's really a common mental shortcut. The idea is that if we are tasked to search for certain objects and we find a shiny object, we lock in; we stop searching.

There is also the media. They could not reach beyond stories that portrayed Beacon as a murderer. Murder involves intrigue, and it sells. One of the medical doctors interviewed by an investigative journalist, Dr. Hugo, later named as an expert for the prosecution, said that Beacon gave enough fentanyl to kill an elephant. This is typical overly dramatic, emotionally laden language of medical experts who are in high demand to testify frequently in malpractice cases. The real Dr. Hugo can be found listed with the Expert Institute, a company that provides medical experts for litigation. The Institute tells experts, "Get hired, get paid." Experts-for-hire are skilled in persuasion and frequently rely on hyperbole to make their points in the courtroom. Of course, plaintiff's lawyers say that defense experts can be just as dramatic in the courtroom. I can neither confirm nor deny that allegation.

Journalists are limited in their reporting, but they could have sought out fair-minded defense attorneys with the proper expertise to assess what was truly at stake, rather than uncritically swallowing public statements by lawyers with a vested interest in the outcome. The local media failed to recognize that the plaintiff's lawyers were posturing and were giddy over the opportunity to plant negative information about Beacon and the hospital that inflated the settlement value of their cases. The local journalist published sound bites of the expert's cherry-picked hyperbole, instead of explaining the fatal realities of patients who would never survive without life support.

It's not clear whether the prosecutor's office got caught up in the media's dramatization of the families' and lawyers' accusations of murder, yet it is not debatable that the prosecutor's office was out of its depth. I began my career in this same prosecutor's office and personally knew a few of the prosecutors primarily responsible for prosecuting this case. They are hardworking, solid lawyers. But even experienced personal injury lawyers refer out medical malpractice cases because of their complexity. Essentially, the Beacon indictments were complex medical malpractice cases that experienced trial attorneys would recognize as requiring a lawyer with extensive experience in medical cases. Lawyers lacking medical expertise are no match for doctors that testify four or five times a year. Special counsel with experience in medical malpractice litigation should have been appointed. And if lawyers with medical expertise had been involved, it is my belief that the hard evidence of the lack of a standard maximum dosage of fentanyl that imposed limitations on its use would have factored heavily against indicting Beacon. Lawyers look for medical standards to measure the appropriateness of a doctor's conduct before lawsuits are filed. And it is highly likely such lawyers would have discounted the validity of the public accusations by the plaintiff's lawyers with a vested interest in the success of the criminal proceedings. And more likely, experienced medical malpractice lawyers would have recognized that ending the life of a patient in organ failure who can't live without life support doesn't fit the usual jury perception of punishable misconduct.

As for malpractice lawsuits serving as a public good to clean up the way the hospital delivered medicine to its patients, the hospital ethically informed patients of their conclusions and made changes to its medication dispensing system before the civil cases were filed. The plaintiffs premised their lawsuits on changing the hospital's practices, despite knowing that changes had already been made.

The hospital attempted to fulfill its obligation to be fair and transparent, but the assumption that the contingent fee lawyers would do the same was misguided. I can think of no better idiom to describe what happened to the hospital and Dr. Beacon than "the road to hell is paved with good intentions." Though most of the plaintiff's lawyers were reasonable and settled rather than continuing to pound the hospital and Beacon, a few lawyers were relentless in their effort to maximize recovery.

People hate nasty, aggressive lawyers out for blood, unless, of course, they themselves are in need of a bulldog lawyer. Do you want namby-pamby, or do you want a badass? A badass gets the best results. The hospital naïvely thought the plaintiff's attorneys would play nice. And it cost this hospital millions of dollars on cases involving patients with little or no real damages, and allowed lawyers to exploit the hospital's coffers in most of the cases where the patient was living on life support or actively dying.

From my perspective, this case went off the rails when Beacon was invited to a meeting about his use of fentanyl with hospital administrators, a meeting canceled without explanation. The opportunity to learn that he was an anesthesiologist by training, familiar with the pain and sedative properties of fentanyl, and that his goal was not to chase the pain of a dying patient but to ensure his patients died a painless death, went unnoticed. Comfort care, not murder, was his intention. His explanations didn't surface until his deposition was taken after the criminal trial. The hospital's, prosecutor's, and media's failures are Exhibit A of a search satisfaction error.

Was Beacon blameless?

No. His mistake is one that haunts every malpractice defense lawyer that has ever sat down to review a doctor's medical charting: poor documentation. If a doctor doesn't document a thought process or a conversation, the plaintiffs will claim it didn't happen, and if the nurse or doctor says they did have such conversations, the lawyers will imply they are lying. The lack of documentation of conversations with family members meant lawsuits against Beacon and the hospital were inevitable.

Allowing nurses to override the medication dispensing system was done for a legitimate purpose—to expedite comfort care to patients—but it was a shortcut inviting systematic abuse that regulatory authorities would sanction immediately. Good intentions won't justify regulatory violations, but it's not the stuff of murder. Local newspaper articles were akin to the Santa Ana winds, sparking litigation and pressing the prosecutor to indict in a case he would never have normally taken. That does not mean the hospital and Beacon would have avoided litigation, but the plaintiff's lawyers would not have had the opportunity to use criminal charges to leverage such huge settlements. It would have eliminated the toxic setting of Beacon defending the malpractice claims against simultaneous accusations of criminal behavior. Without the claims of murder, the value of these cases before a civil jury would not attract experienced malpractice lawyers. By the time the cost of litigation and the lawyer's contingent fee are paid and a possible lien given by Medicare for the money the government wants back, there would be little left for the client. Settlement discussions with families grieving over a lost loved one who are getting less than the lawyer see themselves as getting screwed. There is no other way to put this contentious type of meeting into words.

What can be said of the plaintiff's attorneys mentioned here? In my experience, I have not been involved in a more contentious lawsuit involving a fiercer game of chess in the courtroom. No plaintiff's lawyers I have dealt with have done so much with so little. Unethical? No. But, if there is a lawyer's hall of fame for gamesmanship, Sonny Spees would be one of the inaugural inductees.

What can be said about the 12 jurors viewing the evidence through prisms unique to each of them, created by different levels of education, work-life experiences, and core values filtered by political and religious beliefs? Did they fulfill the prophecy of Thomas Jefferson: "I consider trial by jury as the only anchor ever yet imagined by man, by which government can be held to the principles of its constitution"? Or did they stumble, as predicted by Mark Twain: "The jury system puts a ban on intelligence and honesty, and a premium upon ignorance, stupidity and perjury"?

John Adams, trial attorney and the second president of the United States, proclaimed after his unpopular but successful defense of British soldiers charged in the Boston Massacre: "Facts are stubborn things, and whatever may be our wishes, our inclinations, or dictates of our passion, they cannot alter the state of facts and evidence." I think John Adams gets closest to the reality of the courtroom. I just wish more juries treated facts and evidence the same way.

Except for Beacon, everyone moved on. The prosecutor and attorneys moved on to their next cases. The families collected their money and moved on with their lives. The media is on the hunt for its next story.

Where does Dr. Beacon go to get his life back?

30 Expert Witness Abuse and the *Daubert* Standard

Lesson 30: Federal Rule of Evidence 702 has been amended twice to authorize federal judges to exclude scientific evidence of questionable validity. The latest amendment calls out federal judges for failing to do so. In state court, it's usually an exercise in futility.

I am assuming that most of my readers are unfamiliar with the 1993 case captioned *Daubert v. Merrell Dow Pharmaceuticals, Inc.*[1] Legal scholars touted *Daubert* as the answer to junk science—invalid or unsound science to support theories on legal or political claims (for example, the causes of climate change and claims that birds will die from eating wedding rice). Bear with me for a moment while I condense the *Daubert* analysis for the admission of expert testimony; to be sure, this chapter is not about a *Daubert* factor analysis.

Before *Daubert*, *Frye v. United States*[2] established the rule for admissibility of expert opinions on scientific evidence. The standard required general acceptance of the methodology within the relevant scientific community. Mr. Frye was charged with second-degree murder and moved to admit the results of a lie detector test into evidence. The court denied

1. 509 U.S. 579 (1993).
2. 293 F. 1013 (D.C. Cir. 1923).

the motion because the "systolic blood pressure deception test has not gained such standing and scientific recognition among the physiological and psychological authorities." Then in 1991, Peter W. Huber, a graduate of MIT and Harvard Law School and senior fellow at the Manhattan Institute, authored *Galileo's Revenge: Junk Science in the Courtroom.*

In 1993, the U.S. Supreme Court penned the decision outlining the criteria for federal judges to follow when determining the admissibility of scientific opinion. They are: whether the technique or theory can or has been tested; whether it has been subjected to peer review or publication; what is its known or potential rate of error; the existence of standards and controls governing the theory's application; and the time-honored general acceptance test within the relevant scientific community. In 2000, Federal Rule of Evidence 702 was amended to codify and embody the elements in *Daubert,* including two successive cases referred to as the *Daubert* trilogy. Twenty-three years later, Federal Rule of Evidence 702 was amended again. According to legal scholars writing on the amendment, federal judges were found lacking in the application of the rule to exclude questionable expert witness testimony.[3] "The article concludes by calling on Judges to embrace their gatekeeping obligation and to faithfully apply the text of Rule 702 over any obsolete case law to the contrary."

Why were judges, especially federal judges, not applying *Daubert* to exclude expert opinions based on questionable methodology? Because exclusion of the expert, especially in plaintiff's cases, either eviscerated the lawsuit or led to dismissal. Without a causation expert, the plaintiffs could not satisfy their burden of proof. In state court, there was less success than in federal court, because state court judges did not have the time or multiple law clerks on staff to review complicated scientific evidence in *Daubert* motions. Federal court judges usually cherry-pick law school graduates with spectacular academic credentials who can parse through technical data and the science behind expert opinions. In my experience in state court, I had no success filing *Daubert* motions, even when we showed the court the opposing expert relied on dubious data. The cop-out for judges was to default to the common law ruling that the experts' opinion went to weight, not admissibility, essentially allowing the jury to decide the validity of the opinion and leaving the questionable

3. See Mark A. Behrens & Andrew J. Trask, *Federal Rule of Evidence 702: History and Guide to the 2023 Amendments Governing Expert Evidence,* 12 Tex. A&M L. Rev. 43 (2024).

validity of the evidence up to the cross-examination skills of the opposing lawyer.

I had written on *Daubert* in the past during *Daubert* hearings, and I have to confess that I shamefully sprinkled my law review article or subsequent offerings on the arguments to counsel and the court. Of course, no one seemed moved by my brilliance.

Here is an example of how difficult it is for judges to dismiss an expert's opinion on causation that is critical to the survival of the litigant's case. As is true for many of the names of doctors, lawyers, and patients mentioned in this book, they are fictitious. Erin was 18 years old, 36 weeks pregnant, and at five-foot-two inches, weighed 240 pounds. She was induced because of elevated protein levels in her urine. Pregnant women have a higher volume of circulating blood, which can stress organs and cause kidney damage. Her first stage of labor progressed slowly, but in a reasonably safe amount of time. Her second stage stalled at the very end and delivery was assisted with forceps. The infant's Apgar score, the standard scoring system for a baby's physical well-being immediately after birth, was in the normal range. Only minimal resuscitation was necessary. The baby did well for the first 24 hours, but on the second day of life, the baby suffered seizures, and days later an MRI showed brain damage. The plaintiffs claimed there were warning signs that the baby was not getting enough oxygen during the second stage of labor and a C-section was indicated, and if done, would have avoided the child going through life with cerebral palsy.

Dr. Winbush, the plaintiff's primary causation expert, testified in a discovery deposition that during labor, excessive contractions of the uterus caused extreme pressure on the fetal skull, which in turn caused intense pressure on the fetal brain that dangerously reduced blood flow to the brain. The diminished blood flow caused brain cells to die. His theory is called "cranial cerebral compression ischemic encephalopathy." This causation theory is widely known in the microenterprise of brain-damaged baby cases, but not in obstetrical hospital suites or neonatology intensive care units. Instead, this theory winds its way into the courtroom at the behest of plaintiffs suing for medical malpractice. The easy malpractice theory is "if only the doctor would have done a C-section, we wouldn't be here today."

We filed a *Daubert* motion. We argued that Dr. Winbush's theory failed to meet all four criteria of the *Daubert* standard. It was not generally accepted in obstetrics or neonatology; it had not been published in a peer-reviewed journal; the method cannot be tested (ethical considerations would prevent duplicating brain damage for testing purposes); and there is no known rate of error. Dr. Winbush argued that his causation theory had been published. A deep dive into his claim revealed that he had written a chapter in a book published by a publisher of a dubious reputation, not a mainstream medical publisher, and one of our experts stated that this theory had never been submitted to a vetting specialist in a peer-review setting or in medical journals or lectures to members of the American Congress of Obstetricians and Gynecologists. We submitted a portion of a chapter of a medical text authored in part by a nationally recognized obstetrical expert that made the point that this theory only surfaced in lawsuits against obstetrical physicians in cases where plaintiffs claim that earlier delivery would have avoided a newborn's brain injury. In addition, we submitted a decision by a federal judge excluding the head compression theory because it failed to satisfy *Daubert* criteria.

So, we figured the plaintiff's case would end with the court's decision. Our judge was a no-nonsense judge and ran a procedurally tight courtroom. We assumed incorrectly.

There are many reasons that judges deny motions other than on the merits that seriously affect the outcome of a case, and especially on the eve of trial. Chief Justice Rehnquist, in his concurring and dissenting opinion in *Daubert*, raised his concern about turning judges into "amateur scientists." I am assuming that Chief Justice Rehnquist feared that the application of novel scientific principles may not be, as they say, "their cup of tea." I agree, but I don't have an alternative solution. It's no different than a high school guidance counselor advising students about choosing a major in college. Some students will excel in chemistry and engineering, while others would perform better in academic courses such as political science or English lit. Students in both majors may end up as judges. In my opinion, judges at the state level don't have the time, the staff, or the resources to dive into statistical analysis and apply confidence ratios and know the difference between randomized double-blind studies and anecdotal medical literature. One medical research study passes for science and the other is purely an observation by a specialist. The intellectually incapable? It's a problem, but speaking out on this mental deficiency is interpreted as a resentful, unethical attack on the judiciary. We ask a lot of judges and juries when it comes to science in the courtroom, but there is no other way. So what to do when it comes to excluding an expert that you believe is a blowhard?

Research reveals that at the state court level, more times than not, *Daubert* motions are unsuccessful.[4]

Thus, we must consider the consequences of filing a motion that will not achieve the stated objective. An unsuccessful *Daubert* motion will educate your opponent—specifically, give the opposing expert a heads-up on your expert's basis of opinions, allowing for extensive literature reviews to counter your expert's opinions. But, as discussed in earlier chapters, some judges take sides. And the U.S. Supreme Court has reminded trial judges they have complete freedom to do as they wish. As Chief Justice Rehnquist famously put it in *General Electric Co. v. Joiner*,[5] "Nothing in either Daubert or the Federal Rules of Evidence requires a district court to admit opinion evidence which is connected to existing data by the *ipse dixit* of the expert." *Joiner* is part of the *Daubert* trilogy cited for exclusion of expert opinions because of an analytical gap between the data and the experts' opinions. The objection here is directed to the nationally recognized expert with unassailable credentials, or a highly experienced expert who provides an opinion on weak data, like animal studies, for example. In this setting, just because the expert says "I said so" is not enough. As any experienced trial lawyer knows, expert opinions usually come down to "this is the way I see it" when a standard of care or causation opinion is given. The argument of the analytical gap between data and opinion can be raised in most opinions.

The decision to file a *Daubert* motion goes back to one of the ironclad rules of trial practice: Know your judge. Given that a double-edged sword is wielded in just about every case, a *Daubert* motion, though unsuccessful, may provide the filing attorney the opportunity to better understand the basis of the opposing expert's opinions and gather data and evidence that effectively counters the expert's opinion in the courtroom. Whatever is decided, potential consequences should be examined thoroughly.

---

4. See Monica Lynne Coscia, *"Trust Me, I'm a Doctor": Medical Malpractice as a Daubert-Free Zone*, 108 Georgetown L. J. 1761–1814 (2020).

5. 522 U.S. 136 (1997).

31 Notes of Persuasion

Lesson 31: Of all the factors that control the outcome of a trial, the human element may be the most important, in not all, but many of your cases.

I started writing this book before the COVID-19 pandemic. I fancied a memoir, opening the eyes of the general public—and potential jurors—to the tactics and strategy that distract jurors. Juries are tasked with finding facts. The challenge I soon learned is that lawyers engage experts to throw assumptions and opinions at juries, which makes *believability* a major function of the fact-finding process. When it comes to persuasion in the courtroom, "always" and "never" are words (adverbs) that are seldom appropriate on what to do and what not to do when attempting to influence a jury. Sometimes in my trials, both as a plaintiff's lawyer and a defense lawyer, juries ignored medical science and logic. *Why?* I wondered. In hindsight, it's my belief that the human element plays an important role in jury decisions. Jurors want to do the right thing, but the right path depends on how a person sees the world. Do they believe that doctors are doing the best they can when making decisions based on incomplete information and uncertainty, or do they believe that when something bad happens, someone must be to blame? Does their work-life experience predict their belief in personal responsibility, or do their economic circumstances suggest they could use a helping hand? A bad experience sticks with a person; an adverse reaction to a drug may cause a person to reject future treatment or anyone associated with treatment of the medical illness (vaccines come to mind).

There is no surefire way to avoid placing people on a jury that no amount of evidence will persuade to accept your version of the truth. But in recent decades, a thorough voir dire is the best approach. A major problem here is judges who want lawyers to get on with it and pick the jury fast, with the usual questions. And there is little a lawyer can do with jurors that harbor negative feelings about your case, but sit silent. As a young trial lawyer, when jurors rejected my analysis of the limitations of labs and testing and a physician's mental capability to figure out how to intervene and check the progress of a disease, I never truly knew why. Yet after 50 years of trying, I believe the problem is multifaceted: cultural values, cognitive failures, and emotional and intellectual readiness. Some of us are not committed to patiently listen and understand technical information. How does one persuade individuals who don't understand or who don't listen? In the courtroom, that is a tough assignment. We lawyers think we are the most important person in the courtroom. Jury consultants say otherwise. Getting jurors who align with your client's circumstances and challenges provides the best chance of a favorable jury verdict.

In the preceding chapters, I have sought to show why reasoning plummets down a rabbit hole in the setting of a trial, where lawyers try to motivate people to accept the truth and reality of the cause and effect of treatment of a disease or illness. There is a virtual consensus shared by lawyers, as well as jury consultants, that jurors start leaning toward one side or the other after the lawyers deliver their reasons why in their opening statement, before they hear any evidence. And trial lawyers know from experience that before final arguments, many of the jurors have already decided who to believe. My goal is to encourage lawyers to recognize that in the courtroom, human nature is the elephant in the room. My advice to witnesses before they take that fretful walk to the witness stand is "It's not what you say, it's how you say it."

The quote by Will Durant, "Nature has never read the Declaration of Independence," changed my approach to preparing for trials. Human nature has never been fair. Trial attorneys should seek a fair trial, but don't be foolish enough to expect you'll get a fair-minded judge and jury. Radiology sharpened my insight into cognitive failure and why we make mistakes. One of my goals is encouraging lawyers to take a moment to educate jurors to at least consider whether what they hear or read is factual, or simply a self-serving assumption masquerading as an opinion. The fork in the road at any level of a trial is the difference between errors made because of human imperfection, which hopefully is forgivable, as opposed to careless or negligent conduct.

Now for the bad news.

Having spent my entire professional life trying to simplify complex medical concepts for consumption by people without any medical training, the pandemic taught me that well-explained scientific explanations by highly specialized physicians are just as likely to be rejected as my feeble attempts to persuade jurors to accept my version of the truth. The mistrust of science has been around since the 15th century, when Copernicus came up with the crazy idea that the earth revolved around the sun. The Catholic Church rejected his theory as absurd. Likewise, the pandemic would prove to be the perfect gauntlet for the decline in confidence of medical and scientific explanations by experts on the virus and vaccines. I don't think I truly understood this mindset until I received the jury consultant's report in Brian Manning's cancer case. I submit that purely relying on a medical explanation of treatment outcomes in diseases or illnesses to convince the jury of your theory of liability or defense of a doctor is risky. In broader terms, science and logic are necessary, but can't be depended on to persuade juries.

During the pandemic, doctors and medicine were challenged and at times rejected. For some people, facts, logic, and unassailable experts failed to alter their belief in "easily disprovable facts." Dr. Lisa Rosenbaum, an Assistant Professor at Harvard Medical School and a practicing cardiologist, describes a phenomenon called *biased assimilation*: "When doubt is wrapped up in one's cultural identity or powerful emotions, facts often not only fail to persuade, but may further entrench skepticism."[1] In her opinion, the rejection of science is not a problem rooted in intellect. Resistance, she asserted, has little to do with lack of education and more to do with dismissing facts that threaten one's identity or beliefs. I must confess that I disagree in part with her on the lack of education, not a roadblock to understanding. I think closed minds have something to do with the lack of perspective, in the sense of a failure of curiosity, a failure to think outside the box, to borrow a tired idiom, or to grasp the unpleasant realities of medicine and scientific truths. But my wife says that I'm just frustrated by people who don't agree with me. Maybe so,

1. Lisa Rosenbaum, MD, *Resisting the Suppression of Science*, 376 NEJM 17 (2017).

but if you're a trial lawyer, it's your job to get jurors to reach and understand beyond their personal experience and knowledge.

One more thing: Expert witnesses, many times, are simply ignored by jurors. On the defense side, many times we have brought to court the leading authorities on the study and treatment of a medical issue, only to hear from jurors after the trial that the expert's opinions were not considered. It is a challenge for many experts to tell a story about patient care, but science, wrapped up in the personal story of the doctor's frustration in the fight to save patients, sometimes touches the hearts of jurors. That can be persuasive.

So does that mean that what I have written here is of no consequence? That we really can't change people's minds? No. I believe that we make many decisions daily that require us to question the assumptions upon which opinions are rendered, many of them unrelated to our cultural identity. But what can be done about those individuals who are dismissive of evidence that threatens their core values, and for whom more evidence only widens the gap between self-absorption and reality? Outside the courtroom, we will have to look to behavioral psychologists for solutions to undo biased assimilation. Inside the courtroom, I have seen jurors suspend their personal biases and prejudices and compromise when the facts believed by the majority bump up against their personal beliefs. I have seen jurors cry when their verdict is announced in open court. I know they have been persuaded by the majority, and though it hurts, they have changed their mind.

It takes courage to sit on a jury and judge another human being. Some lawyers raise the issue of courage during jury selection. In medical malpractice cases, the jury's decision will either hurt the patient or the doctor. There is no other way. It takes courage to rise above one's partisan beliefs and reach a verdict antithetical to personal values. Psychologists say that courage is an inextricable component of resilience. The historian Will Durant said, "Forget mistakes. Forget failure. Forget everything except what you are going to do right now. And do it." I don't claim to be as insightful as Will Durant, but my experience tells a different story. Human beings don't forget. They carry their baggage with them every day, affecting their judgment. It's a bitter pill to swallow when jurors slap you in the face and side with your opposition. Trial lawyers embrace defeat at the hands of a jury, whine for a few days, get back on their feet, stand up in the courtroom, and fight again for their clients. It's what we do; we help people who can't fight for themselves. Keep fighting for what you believe is right. But if you fail, and you likely will at one time or another, you're not a failure. Remember, human nature doesn't believe in a fair fight. It takes sides. Unless you cross the line of ethical conduct, getting on the right side of human nature may be the best you can do for your client.

Closing

I've been trying cases for more than 50 years now. Along the way, I've read many books about lawyers and judges hoping to find the secret sauce explaining how to be a great trial lawyer—not just good, but the kind who can humble a windbag witness or mesmerize a jury in final arguments. Some of those books are listed in the bibliography. Truthfully, I never found a book, article, or lecture that gave me a roadmap to excellence in the courtroom, though I found many to be inspirational. As a young lawyer I listened to every taped lecture by Irving Younger, the consensus cross-examination guru in the 1970s and 80s. Today, we still hear about one of Younger's ten commandments on cross-examination: A lawyer should never ask a question he doesn't know the answer to. Good advice, but what I learned after many a harpoon chucked by a hired gun on the witness stand is that it's not what I know about the truth; it's what part of the truth I can force the witness to concede. Just because I know what the answer should be doesn't mean the witness will give me the answer I expect. There is a caveat here that took me a long time to come to grips with: Unless I was ready to impeach the witness, the hurtful answer would linger with the jury. The lesson here is that evasive witnesses rarely answer truthfully. Impeachment is the lawyer's only hedge against erronious testimony.

Human nature stumbles when it looks for the truth. In this imperfect world, with imperfect people, people with limited education, stunted mental acuity, people with egotistical instincts, people with selective memory, and witnesses who proliferate different versions of the truth, all of these flaws in the human condition must be anticipated. When I began this journey as a trial lawyer, I assumed doctors under oath would answer questions honestly. I learned that if the question zeroed in on the fundamental theory—the heart of the opposition's claim—the answers were evasive. Very bright clients sitting next to me at the counsel table would lean over to me and say, "Ask him this question; it's in the medical literature, he won't deny it." I wouldn't ask, because I didn't trust paid experts to concede a point that undermines or contradicts their opinions.

So, is there a secret sauce to becoming a great trial lawyer? There may be, but there is not one recipe. However, there are a few common ingredients. (And don't forget, great trial lawyers still lose cases.)

First, trial work is a skill business, which means unless you are a child prodigy, commitment to the craft, and experience is an absolute necessity.

Second, reasonable intellect is necessary, but so is emotional intelligence. MBA programs call this a soft skill. I call it reading the room. Do not make a witness cry on cross-examination. Don't make jurors hate you.

Third, likeability comes into play in the courtroom. The lawyer's gender, age, or color of their skin are inconsequential. It helps if you enjoy conversing with strangers, but an offensive personality, arrogance, or snarky comments turn off jurors—not a good thing when the goal is persuasion. The problem of talking down to the jury or giving a lecture usually arise with experts, get rid of them, and an absolute no-no for lawyers.

Fourth, should you believe jurors when they say they can be fair? No—they may try but unchecked human nature is inherently unfair. Jurors won't follow jury instructions that impugn their core values.

Fifth, in the past, lawyers were taught to give the jury a "bird's eye view of the case." Opening statements only presented the facts of the case, not arguments and opinions. Today, lawyers deliver their opening statement in story form. Stories have more persuasive effects than facts and logic. A notable example of the facts told in story form is the prosecutor's opening statement in the movie *My Cousin Vinny.* His opening statement takes about two and half minutes to watch on YouTube. Opening statements are a critical time to persuade jurors—by telling a compelling story.

Sixth, practice ethically and if possible, find a good mentor. Sharp practice, as it was called back in the day, is not unethical but conduct that exceeds accepted courtesies and standards of practice eventually come back at you.

Seventh, well-prepared lawyers developed their roadmap of the evidence around one or two theories in their case in chief. Jury selection, opening statements, and testimony of the witnesses are tailored to the theories in the case. Evidence that does not fit or advance your theory should be ignored during your case in chief.

Eighth, trial work requires skill, and the most important skill is the lawyer's execution of his performance in the stressful environment of the courtroom. Two sports figures come to mind. Vince Lombardi once said that there were eight or nine ways to block a dive play—for the uninitiated, that's a quick running play where the running back charges the line of scrimmage. The key to success, Lombardi added, is execution—perfect performance of the blocking scheme chosen. It didn't matter which one. The second sports figure is former heavyweight champion Mike Tyson, who said, "Everyone has a plan until they get punched in the face." Trial lawyers must perform at a high level in a stressful, combative environment without losing their thinking cap. Something always comes up at trial that even the most well-prepared lawyer may not anticipate, such as an unanticipated objection or ruling or a witness faltering, but you must maintain your cool.

Ninth, in civil cases where money is the issue, the most important witness is your client. If your client is seeking damages, the jury must feel that your client is worthy of their help. In my experience, this means the jury must *like* your client, empathize with your client, and want to make your client's life better. Transporting the jury into the shoes of your client motivates them. Remember, it is inappropriate to ask jurors to stand in your client's shoes, but that is exactly what you want them to do. As for defendants such as doctors and professionals, the jury must take the side of your client. Likability is key, but it is imperative that your client is perceived as doing the best he could, even in the most demanding situations. I believe that juries will overlook mistakes if they like the defendant and believe she did her best under the circumstances.

Tenth, if you choose to take on injury cases and lose—whether advocating for a severely injured plaintiff or defending a professional whose hard-earned reputation from years of dedication and sacrifice is permanently erased by a jury after a few hours of deliberation—these losses stick with you. When I look back on my career, my mind seems to skip over the wins. It's the cases I lost that I remember (I should say that haunt me). I've tried to embrace failure and learn from it. Don't sulk over your losses for more than a week.

Eleventh, the difficult judge. I am not talking about a judge who gets one or two rulings wrong. It's the judge who can not put aside thier liberal or conservative views. and worse, those judges who suffer from the Dunning-Kruger Effect. Judges who "insist they possess knowledge and skills they obviously do not." No amount of case law or logic is persuasive. All one can do is be firm, make your record and do not openly criticize the judge except to trusted friends. Criticism will find its way back the judge. The older I get the harder it is to follow my own advice.

Twelfth, there are two kinds of trial lawyers: lawyers who win a case they thought surely they would lose, and lawyers who lose a case they were confident they would win. Half of the time, the loser looks for someone or something to blame. The winner of a nail biter sprints for the exit before a juror changes his or her mind. The thrill of winning and the cost and shame of losing is all part of a career in the courtroom. To paraphrase Hyman Roth, consoling Michael Corleone after a close friend was killed by a rival Mafia family in *The Godfather: Part II*: "This is the business we've chosen." In the long run, every lawyer and judge is hated by someone.

Thirteenth, we lawyers tell our selves that we are in the buisness of helping people especially those who can't help themselves or clients that have made a mess of their life or buisness. But given the nature of the adversary process, we ruffle feathers—we hurt people. In the long run you will be hated by someone. Despite how much you tell yourself you have a client to represent and everyone is entitled to representaion, you'll be the skunk at the lawn party . . . except when your critics need a bad ass lawyer.

If you are interested in the secret sauce for great trial lawyers, ask yourself this question: are you the Michael Jordan of trial lawyers? Consider what Jordan said about sucess: "I've missed more than 9000 shots in my career. I've lost almost 300 games. 26 times I've been trusted to take the game-winning shot and missed. I've failed over and over again in my life. And that is why I succeed."

BIBLIOGRAPHY

You already know this: I do not have a book club and I am not on the Pulitzer Prize board for non-fiction. I have read all of these books. Some of them I believe are informative and provide insight into the challenges of trial practice. I have placed an asterisk next to those books I believe add some insight into the skill set of trial lawyers.

Dan Abrams & David Fisher – *Lincoln's Last Trial*

F. Lee Bailey – *To Be A Trial Lawyer*

Preet Bharara – *Doing Justice*

Robert P. Burns – *Death of the American Trial**

Johnnie Cochran – *A Lawyer's Life*

Alan Dershowitz – *Letters to a Young Lawyer*

Brian Dirck – *Lincoln the Lawyer*

Ward Farnsworth – *The Legal Analyst: A Toolkit for Thinking About the Law**

John A. Farrell – *Clarence Darrow: Attorney for the Damned*

Noah Feldman – *Scorpions*

Robert A. Ferguson – *The Trial in American Life**

Lawrence M. Friedman – *The History of American Law*

John Grisham – *The Innocent Man: Murder and Injustice in a Small Town*

Jonathan Harr – *A Civil Action**

Oliver Wendell Holmes, Jr. – *The Common Law*

Daniel Kahneman – *Thinking, Fast and Slow** (Every lawyer should read this book.)

Rebecca Love Kourlis & Dirk Olin – *Building Justice: Civil Courts in Jeopardy and Why You Should Care*

Harper Lee – *To Kill a Mockingbird**

Paul M. Lisnek – *The Art of Lawyering: Essential Knowledge for Becoming a Great Attorney*

Paul M. Lisnek – *The Hidden Jury**

Antonin Scalia, Bryan A. Garner – Making Your Case – *The Art of Persuading Judges**

Stuart M. Speiser – *Lawsuit*

Gerry Spence – *How to Argue and Win Every Time*

Brian Stevenson – *Just Mercy**

Evan Thomas – *The Man to See: Edward Bennett Williams Ultimate Insider; Legendary Trial Lawyer*

Jeffrey Toobin – *Opening Arguments (A Young Lawyer's First Case: United States v. Oliver North)*

Jeffrey Toobin – *The Nine: Inside the Secret World of the Supreme Court*

Jeffrey Toobin – *The Run of his Life: The People v. O.J. Simpson**

Lawrence H. Tribe – *God Save this Honorable Court*

Scott Turow – *One L*

Francis Wellman – *The Art of Cross-Examination**

Curtis Wilkie – *The Fall of the House of Zeus: The Rise and Ruin of America's Most Powerful Trial Lawyer**

Jill Wine-Banks – *The Watergate Girl**